BABALAWO
SANTERIA'S HIGH PRIESTS

© Elizabeth Felix-Discussion

About the Author

Frank Baba Eyiogbe has been practicing Santería for over twenty-seven years: twenty-three years as a santero (Orisha priest) and eighteen years as a babalawo (initiated in Cuba). Frank has achieved the highest level of babalawo, "Olofista." He created the premier Santería website www.or-ishanet.org and has been a guest on NPR's *All Things Considered* and *The Global Guru* and was interviewed for *LIFE* magazine. He has guest lectured at the University of Washington as well as UC Berkeley.

BABALAWO

SANTERÍA'S HIGH PRIESTS

FATHERS OF THE SECRETS IN
AFRO–CUBAN IFÁ

FRANK BABA EYIOGBE

Llewellyn Publications
Woodbury, Minnesota

FIRST EDITION
First Printing, 2015

Cover design by Kevin R. Brown
Cover illustration: Rudy Gutierrez; additional images: iStockphoto.
   com / 8464821 / ©Axusha
Editing by Jennifer Ackman

All photographs in this book were taken by Frank Baba Eyiogbe except
the photo of Tata Gaitán in chapter 12, page 175, is courtesy of David Brown, and
the photo of Pete Rivera in the epilogue, page 184, is courtesy of Angel L. Rivera.

Llewellyn Publications is a registered trademark of Llewellyn Worldwide Ltd.

Library of Congress Cataloging-in-Publication Data
Eyiogbe, Frank Baba.
   Babalawo, Santería's high priests : fathers of the secrets in Afro-Cuban ifá / by Frank
Baba Eyiogbe. — First Edition.
      pages   cm
   Includes bibliographical references and index.
   ISBN 978-0-7387-3961-8
   1. Santería. 2. Ifá (Religion) 3. Babalawos. I. Title.
   BL2532.S3E95 2015
   299.6'74—dc23
                        2014037048

Llewellyn Worldwide Ltd. does not participate in, endorse, or have any authority or responsibility concerning private business transactions between our authors and the public.
   All mail addressed to the author is forwarded but the publisher cannot, unless specifically instructed by the author, give out an address or phone number.
   Any Internet references contained in this work are current at publication time, but the publisher cannot guarantee that a specific location will continue to be maintained. Please refer to the publisher's website for links to authors' websites and other sources.

Llewellyn Publications
A Division of Llewellyn Worldwide Ltd.
2143 Wooddale Drive
Woodbury, MN 55125-2989
www.llewellyn.com
Printed in the United States of America

For Elizabeth Felix-Discussion (Oloyú Omó Obá),
the greater half of the calabash of my existence.
Apetebí Iború, Apetebí Iboya, Apetebí Ibocheché

Acknowledgments

First and foremost I want to thank my beloved wife and *apetebí* Elizabeth Felix-Discussion (Oloyú Omó Obá). This book could never have existed without you, your patience with my interminable hours of writing and endless first drafts, and your constant care when I was ill. Your love, support, and belief in this book made it possible. I owe you a dream vacation.

To our precious *ibeyis* (twins), Xochitl (Obá Omá) and Emiliano (Alamitó): you two are the light of my life. More than anything, this book is for you.

To my Oluwo Siwayú (padrino) Pete Rivera (Odí Ogundá): You brought me into the world of Ifá, a gift truly beyond measure and price. Your *oddun* allows you to initiate only two babalawos. It was my great good fortune that you chose me to be one of those two. You were like a second father to me, and you taught me how to work in a world of *aché*, and you don't necessarily have to do anything big or complex to achieve tremendous results. I couldn't ask for a better padrino.

To my oyugbona Miguelito Perez Alvarez (Ogbe Dandy): your immense wealth of knowledge of Ifá and your patience with my endless questions made me the babalawo I am today. I am immensely proud to be your godchild. Thank you and Padrino Pete for helping me realize my childhood dream: to learn the secrets of the universe.

To my padrino Guillermo Diago (Obá Bí): You taught me hard. You taught me well. And I will be forever grateful to you. Ibaé bayé tonú (rest in peace).

To all three of my padrinos: most of what is in this book, and most of what I know, I learned at your feet. The mistakes are mine.

My thanks go to all the babalawos I have had the privilege of spending time with inside and outside the *igbodún* (initiation room), whether in Havana or in the United States. I'm afraid to name any of you because I know I would forget someone important, but you know who you are.

I would also like to thank Elysia Gallo, senior acquisitions editor at Llewellyn, for taking a chance on a first-time writer. You made a monumental task so much smoother through your encouragement, patience, and timely advice.

Contents

Notes on the Writing of This Book

There are a number of protocols I have followed in this book that I feel should be explained, including the names of the religion and of priestesses and priests, the spelling of Lucumí terms, and the use (or lack thereof) of the names of *odduns* (divination signs) associated with the stories and proverbs found in this book.

What's in a Name?

The religion most people know as Santería is also known as *La Regla Lucumí* (The Rule of the Lucumí), *La Regla Ocha* (The Rule of Ocha or Orichas), or simply *Lucumí, Ocha,* or *La Religion* (The Religion). Lucumí was originally the term used for people brought to Cuba from the various African nations, now known as the Yoruba. These days some in the religion take exception to the term Santería as they believe it implies our religion is much more syncretic than it actually is or because they feel the term is a reminder of slavery times. In actuality, the Catholic saints were used to hide the *orichas* (goddess or god), and there was very little mixing of the two religions at all. *Santeras* and *santeros* are also known as *iworos* or *olorichas* (an oricha priest), words denoting priest and one who has an oricha. And as we will discover in chapter 3, the early Lucumís deliberately subverted Christianity to fit their own needs, using only the aspects of the Western religion that suited their own needs and worldview.

Names of babalawos are followed by their oddun in Ifá in parentheses; for example, Pete Rivera (Odí Ogundá) or Miguelito Perez Alvarez (Ogbe Dandy). Among one another, babalawos often refer to each other by their odduns rather than their names or will combine the two. For instance, I am often called Frank Baba Eyiogbe or simply Baba Eyiogbe.

Olorichas (santeros) have the names given to them by their oricha during their initiation in parentheses after their names: i.e., Guillermo Diago (Obá Bí-ibae). The word *ibae* is often used here for priests who have passed away. This is our equivalent to "rest in peace" in English.

Language

Many of the terms in this book are in a language called Anagó or Lucumí, a language developed in Cuba that evolved from the Yoruba language. Anagó is a liturgical language, used mainly in prayers, songs, and religious terms. Unfortunately, very few people are able to speak the language conversationally anymore. The tongue is partially a mix of the different dialects slaves brought to the island, with the Oyó and Egbado dialects having the greatest influence. Some of the words come from *oró iyinle* (deep words), which are archaic forms of speech used by the old priests, and often the literal meanings of these words are lost in both Cuba and Africa. The Anagó language in many ways has become locked in time to when the slaves came to Cuba, mainly in the nineteenth century.[1]

Yoruba is a tonal language, and one of the most noticeable differences between the Yoruba and Anagó languages is the lack of tones in Anagó due to the influence of the Spanish language, particularly in written forms of the language. Sometimes tones are approximated through the use of accents, but not always. Oricha priests and others often spelled the words phonetically according to the Spanish orthography, and words may be spelled in different ways in different books. For example, the word for two, which I spell here as meyi, may also be spelled meji or melli in a different place. So the spellings used in this book are just one way of spelling these words and are not definitive by any means. Of course, all these factors can make it extremely difficult to match words with modern Yoruba. In recent years some have changed the Lucumí spellings in an attempt to bring them in line with a perceived "correct" Yoruba spelling. This was done because of the acceptance of the mistaken notion that the Lucumí language is nothing more than a degraded form of Yoruba.

I was unable to include a guide to translating words from Anagó to modern Yoruba or vice versa, but those interested in attempting translations between Anagó and modern Yoruba can find a basic guide at www.orishanet.org/translate.html.

A final word on words—I realize some of the terms may be a bit difficult to remember at first for those who are unfamiliar with the region or religion. Therefore, I have tried to make the glossary at the back of the book as complete and informative as possible. In fact, it is complete enough to serve as handy vocabulary for those just getting started in the religion as well. For those people I have also included useful words that are not found in the book but are often used in the religion.

I recall when a popular book was released that had taken a large number of Lucumí songs and translated them to modern Yoruba and then to English. Like a lot of people, I was thrilled at the prospect of having a reference to translations of a number of songs all in one place—until I tried singing one of these corrected songs in front of my padrino Guillermo, that is...

"No, no, no, NO. No es popo fun mi, es popoPÚN mi." My padrino's exasperated tone made it obvious he was not in agreement with such corrections.

Fortunately, I knew enough to realize that it was likely the book that was wrong and not the elder with more than fifty years in the religion. When I delved deeply into one of my older Yoruba dictionaries, there it was. It turns out that *popopún* is a bed or bedding (the song is used when spreading the feathers over the oricha after a sacrifice). The words "popopún mi, popopún mi iyé" translated to "my blanket, my blanket of feathers." When I started looking at the songs in the book with more critical eyes, it became obvious that the author had been so sure of the fact that Anagó was an extremely degraded form of Yoruba that he had drastically changed many of the songs' lyrics to make them fit modern Yoruba. I shelved the book, and I haven't seen it in years. I assume I must have eventually thrown it or given it away. Looking back, I realize the book was extremely valuable after all. That book was the first crack in the popular notion that the language—and, indeed, the religion itself—was merely a degraded version of a pure and correct Yoruba model. Once that crack appeared, it wasn't long before I began to see more and more evidence the Lucumí religion was far less degraded than many people, including myself, thought. Like my first exploration of the popopún song, upon closer and more critical examination, it became clear that far from being degraded, the Lucumí religion had preserved many things that were lost, even in the religion's homeland.

We must also take into account that the Yoruba language did not have a written form until after most of the slaves had already been brought to Cuba. In Africa, the first Yoruba dictionary was not published until 1843, when Christian missionary Samuel Crowther composed it as part of his plan to unite the various Yoruba nations under Christianity. The standard Yoruba seen in most dictionaries is itself a mix of mainly the Egba dialect and Oyó grammar. Like all languages, including Spanish, English, and, yes, the Yoruba language, the Lucumí language has changed and adapted to accommodate influences from a variety of sources during its development. So, for all intents and purposes, just as the Lucumí traditions have developed into their own religion over time, the language of Anagó evolved into its own separate language.

After reading Stephan Palmié's ground breaking piece *The Cooking of History: How Not to Study Afro-Cuban Religion,* I came to the realization that, like it or not, whichever way I spell the words in this book would be a political act. If I used a pseudo-Yoruba orthography, which is Yoruba without the diacritical marks, I would be conceding that the Lucumí language and religion is a degraded form of the Yoruba versions and are somehow in need of correcting, which they are not. So, by using the classic Lucumí orthography taken from the Spanish, as Lucumís have been writing the language for more than a hundred years, I am clearly stating that the Lucumí language and the Lucumí religion are correct just the way they are.

Photos

To take photographs of orichas is considered sacrilege by many people in the religion, and no actual photographs of orichas were taken for this book. All of the receptacles for the orichas and Echu Elegguá used in the photographs are empty and unconsecrated. Even the *ekin nuts* (used in worship and divination) seen in the book are unconsecrated. This way I could give people an idea of how orichas in priests' homes appear without actually photographing the deities themselves.

Odduns

The *patakís* (parables, histories), *refránes* or *owe* (proverbs) in this book all come from the different odduns in Ifá. They are part of our oral tradition that was passed down from my elders, particularly Miguelito Pérez and Pete Rivera, my *padrinos* (godfathers) in Ifá. Versions of some of these patakís and refránes may also be found in Ifá books, such as the various versions of *Dice Ifá* and the *Tratado de Odduns de Ifá* as well.

In the 1940s Pedro Arango published a book called *Iwe ni Iyewó ni Ifá Orunmila*, which gave detailed information on the odduns of Ifá. In his "Words from the Author" section prefacing the second edition of the book, Arango admitted copies of the first edition of the book had fallen into the hands of a woman, presumably a santera, and two *obá oriatés* (master of ceremonies in Ocha). Arango wrote that to save his responsibility, and probably his reputation as well, he was publishing the greatly enlarged second edition using much tighter security. In addition, Arango threatened to publicly denounce to their elders any non-babalawo found to be in possession of the book. In fact, the accessing of books on Ifá odduns by non-babalawos is very likely to have played a major role in the frictions we see today between olorichas and babalawos.

In keeping with tradition, the corresponding odduns to most of the patakís and refránes in this book will not be included, except where the oddun's name is necessary to the context in which the pataki or refrán is being used. While the patakís and refránes themselves are not considered secrets, most traditional babalawos refrain from publicly stating the names of the odduns associated with them. This information is for the exclusive use of fully initiated Ifá priests who have the *aché* (spiritual power) and the authority from Olófin to interpret or work Ifá.

Somos babalawos ... Jurado para ayudar la humanidad
Somos babalawos ... Ifareando en la Habana donde se Ifarea al duro,
sin guantes.
Somos babalawos ...

We are babalawos ... Sworn to aid humanity
We are babalawos ... Working Ifá in Havana,
where they work Ifá the hard way, without gloves.
We are babalawos ...

Introduction

I remember as a young boy looking up at the stars and wishing that I could learn the secrets of the universe. Little did I know that my simple childhood wish would one day lead me not to some exotic form of Eastern mysticism or a career in cosmology or astrophysics but on a flight to Havana, Cuba, where I was to be initiated as a high priest in a religion regarded by many, albeit erroneously, as primitive at best. In other words, I was being initiated as a witch doctor, but as I eventually learned for myself, this particular path was the best road I could have possibly taken to fulfill that wish. The priesthood I was being initiated into turned out to be as profound as any path toward the knowledge of life, the universe, and everything to be found in the world today.

Hidden within the mysterious Afro-Cuban religion commonly called Santería* there is an even deeper body of secrets and rituals known as Ifá practiced by a group of priests known as babalawos, meaning "fathers of the secrets" in the Lucumí and Yoruba languages. For hundreds of years

---

* Though commonly known as Santería, insiders often refer to the religion as La Regla Ocha (The Rule of the Orichas), or La Regla Lucumí (The Rule of the Lucumí), sometimes shortened to simply Ocha or Lucumí. Lucumí was originally the term used in Cuba to describe the West Africans now known as the Yoruba. Later it became used to denote the culture, language, and religion as it was preserved and evolved in Cuba.

these babalawos, who serve as the high priests of the Afro-Cuban religion, have jealously guarded these secrets, which may have already been thousands of years old before enslaved babalawos brought them from West Africa to the shores of Cuba.[1]

Babalawos are initiated into the service of Orunmila (often shortened to Orula), the oricha or deity of wisdom and knowledge, and are the only priests who practice Ifá, the highest and most profound form of divination in Santería. Ifá is probably best known for being a sophisticated and remarkably accurate and effective form of divination, containing within it a system of remedies, but Ifá is much more than merely divination. It is a vast body of knowledge and wisdom covering everything from the human condition to the universe at large, as accumulated and distilled over hundreds, perhaps thousands of years.

Over the last eighteen years as a babalawo, I found the more I learned about Ifá, the more I found myself in awe of its depth, insight, and practicality. While Ifá's philosophical roots are at least as sophisticated and profound as any branch of Eastern or Western mysticism you might compare it to, Ifá differs from many of them in one very significant way. Ifá doesn't attempt to somehow transcend nature or our own selves. Instead we constantly strive to achieve and maintain balance and alignment with our own destinies and with the forces of nature that surround us. In fact, as we shall see, balance and alignment is a core concept in Ifá and enters into everything we do, informing our ethics, our worldview, and our actions in daily life as well as in the rituals we do.

Although Ifá is remarkably complex, with 256 odduns, each with innumerable mythic parables, proverbs, recommendations, and remedies, it is ultimately based on the simplest system in the world; a binary system of ones and zeros much like that used by computers. But Ifá goes much further by concluding that, underneath it all, the very fabric of the universe is made up of these ones and zeros, much like an immense computer program. This is only now being echoed by recent discoveries in modern physics that have given scientists the ability to achieve such breakthroughs as quantum teleportation.

We will also experience Afro-Cuban Ifá as a story of incredible self-sacrifice and determination, which allowed this profound body of knowledge to survive and even flourish against the almost insurmountable odds presented by slavery. In fact, Afro-Cuban Ifá has been preserved so well that the foremost spokesperson for African Ifá, Wande Abimbola, recently acknowledged that it is probable that more of the rituals and prohibitions have survived in Cuba than in our tradition's homeland itself.

This book will not shrink from addressing some of the biggest controversies facing Lucumí religion today including animal sacrifice, the *iyanifá* (female Ifá priest), and the frictions existing between the obá oriaté and the babalawo. Is the practice of animal sacrifice merely a brutal and barbaric holdover expected from a primitive religion, and how does it fit in with our modern, enlightened society? Why are Cuban-style babalawos so up in arms over the emerging practice of initiating iyanifás in Africa? What is the role of women in Ifá anyway? Why is there such animosity between some oriatés (who act as ceremonial master of ceremonies)and babalawos, and what, or who, started it? The answers may surprise you and could possibly change not only the way you look at our practices, but how you see our own modern society as well.

Over the last fifteen years I have received hundreds of questions about Ifá on my website, OrishaNet, either through e-mail or on the forums. I found that, while there were a number of books that talk about Ifá, none of them seem to adequately lead readers to any real depth of understanding Ifá. They either focused on the technical aspects or were overly simplistic to the extreme. On the one hand, most of what exists out there consists of short chapters on Ifá found in general books on Santería, often written by non-initiates and just as often riddled with serious errors. On the other extreme are the technical manuals aimed at practicing Ifá priests, which even many babalawos find difficult to understand fully since much of the information found in these books came from hastily scribbled notes. While some academic works have attempted to go more in-depth, these accounts too often contain their own errors because academics have little or no way of evaluating what information they get from their informants due to the extreme secrecy surrounding Ifá and the limitations of their own understanding of the subject. This eventually led me to realize there is a need for an in-depth view of Afro-Cuban Ifá from the inside that would be accessible to initiates and non-initiates alike.

It is my hope that other babalawos might also find this book useful, as it explores our heritage and *why* we do many of the things we do, as opposed to just how. In my experience I have found that the more we grasp the whys and wherefores of the technical aspects that we have learned, the more Ifá's logic makes sense to us and the more effective we become as babalawos. Or, as Ifá tells us in the refrán, "The babalawo who studies Ifá without thinking about it is ineffectual. The babalawo who thinks about Ifá without studying it is dangerous." Then there is the sheer joy that comes from that moment of enlightenment when the light bulb goes on and we get it. At that moment, the overwhelming complexity seems to fall away, and things we have struggled for years to fully grasp suddenly seem startlingly obvious and self-evident.

At the beginning of each chapter I have used a pataki and a proverb taken from the odduns to lend Ifá's insight to the subject in much the same manner as we use them when consulting Ifá for our clients. You will also find these parables and proverbs sprinkled throughout these pages where I use them to further illustrate and reinforce a number of the concepts presented. In this way I am allowing Ifá to speak for himself and to hopefully give readers a glimpse of the richness and depth that Ifá brings to the table. While these parables and proverbs are an integral part of Ifá, the patakís and refránes themselves are not covered by my vows of secrecy, so everybody is invited to learn from the rich insights gathered from thousands of years of wisdom.

This book exists to help you understand our traditions by pulling away the veil of secrecy surrounding Ifá just enough to reveal exactly what Afro-Cuban Ifá is, how and why it works, and to share a bit of our rich history with you. There are, however, some things I cannot talk about in this book. Like every babalawo, upon my initiation to Ifá I was sworn to secrecy, and I take those vows very seriously. But I believe I can show you some of the inner workings of Ifá without resorting to breaking the confidences shown in me by my elders.[2]

While I have physically been writing for much less time, in a very real way this book has been more than fifteen years in the making as I have painstakingly learned, re-learned, and struggled to truly understand what I have been taught about Ifá. In this journey I have been blessed with the good fortune of having been able to learn from some of the most knowledgeable, kindest, and wisest babalawos and olorichas (oricha priests, santeras, and santeros) in our tradition. This book is really theirs. Any errors are, of course, my own.

Let's begin by taking a look at what Ifá is, how it works, and how Ifá came to exist in Cuba. What did the Yoruba world look like at the time the first babalawo was forcibly torn from that world and transformed into human chattel in fulfillment of a hideous curse inflicted on his own people by an embittered Oyó emperor? What were the extraordinary measures these babalawos were forced to take to re-create Ifá and Ocha (Santería) in an alien and hostile New World?

Chapter One
What Is Ifá?

It was past midnight, and Olófin and Baba Eyiogbe were chatting about the nothingness that was the only existence at the time, and how cold and featureless it was. They were beginning to talk about how it might be time to create the universe when suddenly Oyekun Meyi appeared and broke into the conversation. He had obviously been drinking and was in a terrible state.

Olófin asked why he was so upset and Oyekun Meyi responded dejectedly, "I have lost the Key of Light—the key that will open the door to creation and the universe. It was there when I went to sleep, but when I woke up—" With that, Oyekun Meyi began to wail plaintively.

"No, you did not lose the key," said Olófin, his voice cold and even. "Your brother Baba Eyiogbe took it from you while you were drunk and passed out. I see that you are not capable of carrying out the mission I entrusted you with, so I have given the key to Baba Eyiogbe, and from this day forward he will be first in Ifá and first in everything that exists, and you and all the other odduns shall follow him. And where Baba Eyiogbe is light, you shall be the darkness that follows."

When Baba Eyiogbe had finished his preparations, Olófin ordered Oyekun Meyi to accompany him. Then Baba Eyiogbe produced the Key of Light and inserted it into the lock, and from this burst of light the whole universe rushed forth into the void. And, as decreed by Olófin, Baba Eyiogbe led the way, followed by Baba Oyekun Meyi, and then all the other Meyis after that.

"Wisdom, understanding, and thought are the forces that move the world."

A babalawo and his godchild are at the beach. It is night and they are alone with the sea, a perfect time to do the cleansing they need to do for Yemayá. The bright moon looks down on them through the moist sea air, showing no sign of the huge amount of force she is exerting on the sea, forcing foamy water to retreat farther and farther out with each wave. They set down the bags containing their shoes, towels, and the materials needed for the ceremony a good fifty feet from the waves. Satisfied everything is safe, they proceed.

The babalawo marks the ones and zeros of Yemayá's oddun isalaye, the Ifá sign that will compel her powerful presence, reciting the oddun's *llamada* (call) while pouring molasses over the oddun in preparation for the ceremony. The centuries-old prayer is short but effective. Though the ceremony has barely begun and the tide is supposed to be going out, Yemayá cannot resist the call of her oddun combined with the smell of sweet molasses. The Queen of the Seas comes roaring in with a vengeance, and the Ifá priest and godchild are forced to run madly to grab their bags and shoes before they are washed out to sea...

Ifá just may be the oldest and most powerful spiritual path in existence today. Breathtaking in its depth and scope, Ifá is as much a system of knowledge as it is of divination, philosophy, or religion. As we will see, not only were ancient babalawos able to discover the very fabric of the universe, but they also learned how to access it at will and became able to wield tremendous power as a result.

Worldview

In Ifá, we acknowledge that nature itself is the ultimate source of spiritual power, with each of the orichas ruling over aspects of nature that reflect their personalities and traits. For instance, you can learn a lot about Ochún and her human children by watching the rivers and streams, which share in her nature. Although she always heads to her older sister Yemayá, she does so at her own meandering pace. The cool and refreshing babbling brook expresses her sweetness, but her changeable moods are seen in how quickly this brook can be transformed into a raging flash flood, sweeping away everything in her path with terrifying suddenness. Considered to be the Queen of the Witches, she can be very dark when angered, and her vengeance is truly frightening. Her human children are often very sweet and light, like their oricha mother, but they are capable of great perseverance and can be implacable in their wrath.

In much the same way, fire and thunder express the nature of their owner Changó. Fiery is probably the best way to describe Changó and his children. His beloved *omo* (children) are lively and bright. They share with their father a commanding bearing coupled with a burning intelligence that covers a lot of ground quickly but is often quickly extinguished as the omo Changó loses interest and moves on to more interesting new pursuits. Changó is considered the wrath of *Olófin* (God), and when angered his reaction is immediate, overwhelming, and final, as he favors a scorched-earth policy. Nothing commands immediate attention and fear as when an angry Changó possesses one of his children at a *tambor*, or drumming ceremony, and approaches an attendee, telling them "I will say this only once."

When offended or abused, any of the orichas can mete out harsh punishments, even on their own children, so we all tread carefully. In our tradition, we don't have to wait for the afterlife to receive our just desserts, and stories abound about the consequences of angering the orichas. It all depends on us; hence the saying, "You will either learn to love the orichas or you will learn to fear them."

Like many indigenous worldviews, Ifá experiences everything in the world as being alive, aware, and interconnected. In Ifá, plants, animals, mountains, oceans, and rivers are all conscious in their own way as manifestations of the orichas. Our relationship with nature is an intimate one, where we constantly interact with the world in a familiar yet respectful way. If while driving along we pass over a river, we salute Ochún and ask her permission to pass over her, and if traveling over train tracks, we pay our respects to Oggún, the oricha of iron, blacksmithing, and war.

For us, the orichas are not only forces of nature; they are physically consecrated and received by us. Their *fundamentos* (foundational objects) are born in blood, bathed, fed, sung, and prayed to. The orichas we receive are consecrated stones, ekin nuts, or a *carga*, or load, which becomes inhabited by the oricha. The orichas come to inhabit these objects in the same way we as humans inhabit our physical bodies. Our deities are not mere abstract ideas; they are physically with us and are held, washed, fed, and worked with. Our orichas are not just representations; they are alive and must be treated as such. In other words, they are not an "it," they are a she or he. This is why receiving an oricha is much more than a mere initiation. You are receiving an oricha and are committing yourself to the actual care and feeding of the oricha for life. We regularly refer to the orichas we have received as our orichas, as in "my Obatalá wants to be fed some pears" or "her Obatalá is twenty years older than mine and is stronger and more experienced." The orichas are also manifestations of the odduns, which gave birth to them, and in an emergency a babalawo can work with the oricha directly through the oricha's oddun. The aché to do this comes from Olófin, who is the ultimate source of all the odduns, which is why she must be present at the initiation of a babalawo.

Olófin is our most commonly used name for the Supreme Being. Also known as Olodumare and Olorun (Owner of the other world), Olófin is considered extremely distant and deals with the world almost exclusively through the oricha, and only elder babalawos who have received her physically can work directly with her, and even this is done rarely. Sometimes Olodumare and Olófin are described as a husband and wife team who together make up a calabash, which contains everything in existence. At other times Olodumare, Olófin, and Olorun are pictured as a trinity, with Olodumare being defined as the laws of the universe, Olófin as the creator and acting ruler of the orichas and humanity, and Olorun the aché, or universal energy that powers the universe. Although we sometimes speak of them as separate, in many ways they are different manifestations or paths of the same Supreme Being. We often use these names interchangeably, but we mostly use the name Olófin when we talk about God, as she is the form who is closest to us. As we will see later, under the name Odun, Olófin is female, even though many babalawos believe she has both male and female aspects.

The Way of Ifá

Unlike most Western religions, Ifá does not require faith, and it is not uncommon to hear an elder say they simply don't have faith, which may seem shocking at first. However, simply put, Ifá and the orichas don't need our faith for them to exist or for Ifá to work. We don't need to have faith in the orichas any more than we need to have faith that the sun will rise because, like the sun, the orichas are our constant companions. Our continuous experiences of the orichas and their actions in the world are all the proof we need; therefore, we don't ask people to profess faith as some other religions do. In fact, in Africa some Yorubas tease Christians by calling them *igbabo* (believers).[1]

Ifá is more of a way of life or practice-based religion, and in this sense we are much more like Buddhism or Hinduism than the faith-oriented religions such as Christianity. We interact with our orichas rather than merely worship them in the Christian sense. We have an intimate bond with the orichas with the perpetual give-and-take that is the hallmark of any successful relationship, and as children of the orichas,[2] we adore and respect them as cherished family who just happen to be immensely powerful. Unlike other forms of worship, we are in constant dialogue with our orichas through divination. The orichas speak to us through divination with Ifá and with the *diloggún* (cowrie shells) used by iworos, and we can quickly check whether an offering or ceremony has been accepted through the much simpler *obí* (coconut) divination, which elicits yes and no answers from the orichas. The orichas also communicate with us when they make a personal appearance by mounting or possessing one of their *caballos* (horses), usually during a drumming ceremony commonly called a tambor or Wemilere.

In Santería, there is no secular versus sacred time as in Western religions. We don't have a special sacred time because we spend every moment of every day living in a magical world, surrounded by living forces that are constantly intervening in our lives. The idea that you can have separate times for religious and non-religious activities is simply incomprehensible to us.

Like Buddhism, we are not exclusive, and there are many people in the religion who are involved in other religions as well, and Ifá has no issue with this. People are only asked not to mix the religions and to afford them both the respect of giving each of them their own places in our lives and in our homes.

Divination

Divination is at the core of our religion and almost everything we do revolves around it. Besides telling us our past, present, and future with astonishing detail and accuracy, it is through divination that the orichas communicate their wants and needs and are able to deliver warnings, encouragement, and advice. When a person is seen with Ifá, meaning they had Ifá divination performed for them, Ifá advises the client on the best course of action to take, which rituals or offerings are required, and which orichas to go to for aid. In this manner a person can achieve and maintain proper alignment and balance, both within themselves as well as with the forces that surround us. The concepts of balance and alignment will be discussed in much greater depth in a later chapter.

Along with the wealth of predictions and advice given in these odd-uns lies a system of *ebbós* (remedies) specifically associated with each of the Ifá signs to ensure any good fortune predicted or to prevent any misfortune presaged by the sign. In this manner, the orichas give us the advice we need to help us lead the most fulfilling life possible. The odd-uns have countless patakís connected with them. These stories come from a mythic place beyond time and space, and yet they are happening right now.

From Ifá's point of view, every scenario has been playing out since time immemorial and will keep playing out somewhere, for someone, for all eternity. The trappings and a few of the details may change, but the essence remains the same. For instance, a story may speak of an incident that occurred while a person was riding a horse. Nowadays, the same incident would more likely occur while driving or while on a plane, but other than that the person is living very much the same story. Even though the technology of traveling changes, the basic story is always the same whether the person is riding a horse, a Honda, or a rocket car á la the Jetsons. As the old Ifá proverb says, "Modern dogs chase modern rabbits."

Oral Traditions

Ifá also contains the sum total of our oral tradition, where every detail regarding the orichas and our history, as well as a system of precedents governing ritual and rule, is found. The patakís connected with the od-duns explain how everything we do came about and why. Within the patakís, the origins and the reasons for these rules and rituals are spelled out and codified. Everything passed down about each of the orichas, our religion, and how each ritual is supposed to be conducted and why is included and was born in Ifá's odduns. This became crucial when the slaves were taken from Africa and faced the daunting task of re-creating their religion and their culture in the incredibly hostile world of Cuban slavery. Only in Ifá's odduns could all the information on each of the orichas and our ways be found, and that knowledge was organized in a cohesive whole.

Time and Ifá

In Ifá, our future—and, indeed, the future of the universe, including its demise—has already occurred, and the past, present, and future all exist right now. In the words of Albert Einstein, "The distinction between the past, present, and future is only an illusion, however persistent." If you think about the past, present, and future as if it were a movie on a film reel, the idea makes a little more sense. The beginning, middle, and end are already there on the reel, with each moment being a single frame of that film. Each moment in history and in our lives is already on that reel, even the end of the universe, but the events of the past haven't gone away either. The big bang, the birth of the solar system, and our first real kiss is already there on that reel; we just may not have seen it yet. And Ifá has access to the whole thing.

This doesn't mean that everything in the past, present, and future is written in stone, only that our view that time can only go in one direction is an illusion. For us, time goes in one direction, from the past into the future, never stopping or reversing itself. In the subatomic world, it appears particles can and do go backward and forward in time with impunity, and most physical processes work just as well going backward as forward. So, underneath the events we see around us every day, time exists but is virtually meaningless. In quantum reality, particles are often in several places, on several different paths, and existing in several different times all at once. These particles remain ghostlike until they are observed, then the particle suddenly becomes fixed at one place and one time in what is called the collapse of the Schrödinger wave. This bears a striking resemblance to Ifá, where the past, present, and future have a number of *ona* (paths) they may take, with all of them having an ephemeral, phantom existence until one path is decided on and followed. Each can have an effect on another, even at incredible distances.

Recent experiments have shown something very interesting: you can actually change the past by what you do in the present. In 1978, the physicist John Wheeler came up with an idea for an experiment that would prove quantum weirdness was even weirder than we all thought. His Delayed Choice Experiment would force a particle of light, or photon, to decide to be a particle or a wave and have that decision change the nature of the particle in the past as well. Thirty years later, French physicist Alain Aspect, who seems to take a special enjoyment in proving the creepiest parts of quantum mechanics, successfully performed the experiment in such a way that there could be no doubting the results.

The idea that consciousness plays an interactive role with reality at its most fundamental level is also an important component of the Copenhagen Interpretation of the implications of quantum mechanics, hammered out between some of the greatest minds in physics such as Werner Heisenberg, Neils Bohr, and Wolfgang Pauli. In the Copenhagen Interpretation, considered the most orthodox interpretation of quantum theory, a conscious observer is necessary to cause the Schrödinger wave to collapse, leaving the particle in one place and time. This places consciousness at the center of the equation. In other words, the universe requires the participation of intelligent beings in the extension of the awareness of essential knowledge that makes up reality. The interplay of consciousness and thought enter the picture and place us not at the center of the universe but at least return us to being part of the universe, which classical physics and the materialism that reached its peak in the 1800s denied us.

I believe one of the reasons we see so many scientists rejecting the role of consciousness in quantum mechanics is that it opens the door for people to run wild with the quantum consciousness idea and use it to justify virtually any far-fetched fantasy a person might wish to come up with. The scientific method only allows for what can be directly proven, which is most likely its greatest strength. The addition of consciousness to the fray threatens to allow people to misinterpret quantum mechanics, believing they can create the reality around them with whatever they are thinking at the moment.

So does that mean we can change the past, present, and future at our whim? Not only that, but all this with little or nothing to back it up experimentally? There is a saying in the scientific community that extraordinary claims require extraordinary evidence. Quantum mechanics required extraordinary evidence to be accepted. So it is not surprising that they demand similar proof from those of us who speculate about how much our personal consciousness affects the universe. Unfortunately, it doesn't look like it is quite as simple as creating the reality around us with our every thought, but it does mean that the choices and actions we make now are more far-reaching than we ever suspected. And our *orí* (consciousness), when properly aligned, does indeed play a far greater part in the creation of the world around us than most realize. Finally, it shows that the possibility exists where profound changes can be made to any aspect of the reality in which we live.

Relax: They're Just Ones and Zeros

"It's the simplest system in the world, and the most complete. It's a combination—or series of combinations—between something, the one, and nothing, the zero. The entire universe is made of somethings and nothings. With those two ciphers, worlds can be made and destroyed. But we're now in Orula's province. I cannot tell you any more … All the knowledge that can be had lies between the one and the zero."

—PANCHO MORA[3]

Those familiar with computer programming will instantly recognize the similarities between the odduns, written as a series of ones and zeros, and the binary code, which sits at the core of every computer program. Just as a computer groups eight of these ones and zeros, called bits, into chunks called bytes, Ifá, too, combines eight ones and zeros to make up an oddun, which amounts to an Ifá byte. Does that mean Ifá is an ancient computer? Certainly. But there's more to the story … much more.

In Ifá, everything we see around us in the universe was born in one or another of the odduns, as well as every event or human situation. As we have seen, even the orichas themselves were born in their respective odduns. But what if I told you that lying just beneath our day-to-day reality is a breathtaking world made up entirely of the ones and zeros that comprise those odduns from Ifá? Or that the underlying fabric of the cosmos is a series of somethings and nothings, as if the entire universe were a huge computer simulation? Suddenly we are brought face-to-face with the startling conclusion that Ifá is everything: the trees, the animals, the earth, the air we breathe, even the book you are holding right now. Each and every event that is occurring at the moment has occurred or will occur and is also included in the ones and zeros that make up the odduns of Ifá. What if I also told you modern physics had come to almost exactly the same conclusions about the nature of the universe?

In 1948, Claude Shannon, an electrical engineer working for Bell Labs, discovered a formula to predict the amount of information that could be passed through a phone line. In order to do this, he found he had to measure information in the form of ones and zeros, somethings and nothings. A year later, Shannon took his equation to be reviewed by famous mathematician John von Neumann. When Shannon asked the mathematician what he should name his equation, von Neumann told him he should call it entropy because that was what Ludwig von Bolzmann had called it when he developed the concept that later became known as the Second Law of Thermodynamics. Von Neumann jokingly added that calling his discovery entropy would also help him win arguments because nobody really knew what entropy was.

Entropy, also known as the Second Law of Thermodynamics, explains why if you leave the door open between a hot room and a cold room, you will eventually get two even-temperature rooms. It also tells us that you can't make a perpetual motion machine because you will always end up losing energy in heat. Even a computer has to erase information from its memory to make room for new information. Suddenly, scientists started thinking, what if the thing being lost was actually information?

As computers became more and more powerful, scientists began using them to model their ideas to see if they would work in the real world. But the more scientists looked, the more they found that the computers they used to model the universe worked a little too much like the universe itself. Over time, physicists began to find that the connections between information theory and physics went deeper and deeper, and the deeper they searched, the more the idea made sense.

In the 1960s, the brilliant physicist Rolf Landauer came to the startling conclusion that information is physical, which would eventually lead to a revolution in physics. The more physicists examined the idea, the more they began to find information expressed in these ones and zeros explained a lot of the mysteries of quantum mechanics that had perplexed them for decades.

Suddenly, mysteries such as the Heisenberg Uncertainty Principle, which tells us we can't know exactly where a particle is and how fast it's going at the same time, made perfect sense. You can't know the position and speed of a particle at the same time because you simply can't get two answers from one bit of information. By the 1980s, physicist

John Wheeler, who coined the terms black hole and wormhole, came up with the catch phrase "It from Bit" to describe a universe built on these ones and zeros. Dr. Wheeler said:

> It from Bit. Otherwise put, every "it"—every particle, every field of force, even the space-time continuum itself—derives its function, its meaning, its very existence entirely—even if in some contexts indirectly—from the apparatus-elicited answers to yes-or-no questions, binary choices, bits.

This view of the universe as information has allowed scientists like Seth Lloyd to massage subatomic particles to be used as quantum computers, and has made it possible for Anton Zeilenger in Austria to achieve quantum teleportation, which is the instantaneous transfer of a particle's properties from one place to another. Serge Haroche and David J. Wineland used quantum information theory to develop a means to observe individual subatomic particles without destroying their strange quantum properties, and they were awarded the 2012 Nobel Prize in Physics as a result.

Some scientists have taken the idea even further. The universe seems to be structured like a computer program, and in many ways behaves like one as well. In fact, everything in the universe seems to follow the rules of computer logic. So, if the universe looks like a computer program and acts like a computer program … well, it just might *be* a computer program.

When you sit with the idea for a while, it becomes a tiny bit less shocking. Virtual reality has been around for years, as well as CDs, DVDs, and BluRays, which sound and appear perfectly real but essentially are nothing more than a bunch of ones and zeros slapped onto disks. Anyone who has seen the movie *The Matrix* is now familiar with the idea that people could live in what is effectively an immense computer simulation without knowing it. So the idea that our reality is also based on those ones and zeros may not be such a giant leap after all. It is now well established within the scientific community that underneath everything in the universe—each atom, each electron, each boson, and each quark—there is information in the form of ones and zeros, which is exactly what Ifá has been saying for thousands of years. Beyond that, each oddun, each one, and each zero is alive, aware, and connected to everything else. So we are all connected to everything else in the universe.

According to Ifá and modern physics, everything and everyone is made of ones and zeros just like any computer program, making the entire universe essentially a computer program merrily processing away. Entire galaxies then amount to nothing more than directories in this huge program, and solar systems subdirectories. Among all of this is a subdirectory of a subdirectory of a subdirectory called Earth, and farther down is an itsy bitsy subdirectory. Let's call it humanity. Then in this teeny tiny subdirectory, among billions of other files, are the ones and zeros called me. No wonder we consider our god Olófin to appear extremely distant, vast, and unconcerned.

But wait, we aren't finished yet. Have you forgotten we have something called consciousness that effectively makes us living, breathing, and thinking RAM who are processing information, just like the rest of the universe? Since we are conscious, that means the massive program we call the universe has managed to find a way for a tiny part of the program to become conscious of itself. So now we have this universe program that is conscious of itself.

If that isn't enough, now you have a smattering of inconsequential little files in the program that have somehow succeeded in accessing and using the rest of the program to accomplish their own ends. In other words, we have this massive computer program being hacked by a few of its own tiny, insignificant little files. Using simple tools such as the *opón* Ifá (Table of Ifá) and *ecuele* (divining chain) to access prayers, chants, and rituals that manipulate the groupings of eight ones and zeros that make up Ifá's bytes, or odduns, babalawos have become able to exercise power and knowledge far beyond what should be their place in the universe.

You could say Ifá is the totality of knowledge. Everything that exists in the universe and in our lives was born and is described in Ifá's odduns, and babalawos have been accessing and manipulating the vast program called our universe since time immemorial. And they have been effectively hacking the universe ever since.

Ifá is the handwriting of Olodumare (God), and it is simplicity itself. At its core it consists of just two numbers: one and zero.

Orula's apere, or receptacle

Chapter Two
How Ifá Works

There was a time when Orula lived in a land ruled by the other orichas, who didn't believe in him or in his ability to divine, no matter how well Orula and his assistant, Echu, acted toward them. Therefore, Orula and Echu always lived separate from all of the rest.

Echu took to spying on all of the orichas, learning all of their secrets and reporting back to Orula, who then noted and studied them until he had them all memorized. One day all the orichas came together and challenged Orula to demonstrate the knowledge that he was supposed to be so famous for. Orula paused for a few moments and began to reveal their deepest secrets, their ceremonies, their rituals ... everything. In shock, the orichas came forward and began to prostrate themselves to Orula in respect for his great wisdom.

Afterward, Echu asked Orula to consecrate him as an Ifá priest. Grateful for everything Echu had done, he gladly initiated Echu as a babalawo, and from that day forward Orula always gave Echu a portion of everything he earned.

Owe ni Ifá ipa; Omoran ni imo ...
"Ifá speaks in parables; it is the wise man
that understands Ifá's words ..."

It is a scene that has been played out innumerable times since time immemorial. The babalawo sits on a straw mat, the Table of Ifá, representing the universe, situated between his outstretched legs. He dips his middle finger into a small calabash of cool water and shakes droplets to the ground, a libation to cool and refresh everything touching the process that is about to unfold, including the earth; his road and way; Echu; the orichas; the home; and so on. The babalawo then salutes Olodumare, Olorun, and Olófin, the three manifestations of the Supreme Being, and goes on to invoke the dead, the orichas, and finally Orunmila, entreating him to direct the course of the *osode* (consultation) so the unequivocal truth will be revealed.

Presenting the ecuele to the person's head, shoulders, and chest, he makes a strong, solid connection to the client spiritually and materially. Then, if using the ecuele on the Table of Ifá, the Ifá priest will present the ecuele to the four cardinal points and the center of the Table of Ifá, creating an opening between *aiyé* (earth) and *Orun* (the other world) to access the infinite storehouse of knowledge called Ifá. Thus the Father of the Secrets makes a connection to the source of the client's being, her orí, her innermost consciousness and personal destiny, and to the forces and events affecting her life and her development.

"*Ifá re o, Ifá re o* (Ifá blessings O)." With this call for Orunmila's blessing and aid, the babalawo tosses the ecuele to the center of the Table of Ifá and quickly jots down the pattern of ones and zeros that will not only reveal her past, present, and future but the best course of action to take in order to achieve a fulfilling life. The advice, story, proverbs, and remedies associated with each of these odduns are used by the babalawo to accomplish this task.

As you can see, the actual purpose of Ifá divination is not merely to know the future, but to reveal the true nature of the present path and the proper action to be taken. Ifá is famous for its accuracy and effectiveness, which is why in the religion you will often hear the owe or refrán "Orunmila's word never falls to the floor" from babalawos and oricha priests alike.[1] What is the power behind Ifá, and how does Ifá divination work in practice?

Orunmila, as the *Elerí Ikúin* (Witness to Destiny in Creation), is the only oricha allowed to witness creation and to be given the keys to know the destiny of the universe and everything and everyone in it.

The 256 Ifá odduns are the word of Orula, and through these signs Orula gives us an extremely accurate illustration of our situation as well as the best course of action to take. Orunmila acts as the spokesperson for Olodumare (God) as well as for all of the orichas. As the embodiment of the divination system, we often refer to him as Ifá, and when Olodumare placed Orula in the role of Eleri Ikúín, Ifá became the only oricha who knows our destiny. Orunmila, who personally supervises each Ifá divination session, controls just which of these odduns will come up during an Ifá consultation. Within these odduns lays the entirety of the oral traditions of our religion and the secrets of all the orichas. Thus his priests, the babalawos, are considered the highest authorities on the religion, which is why the worshippers of all the orichas in both Africa and Cuba consult them.

The figures that make up the odduns are comprised of eight ones or zeros written in pairs of four, as in the example below for the oddun called *Oché Fun*:

$$
\begin{array}{cc}
\multicolumn{2}{c}{+} \\
0 & 1 \\
1 & 0 \\
0 & 1 \\
1 & 0 \\
\end{array}
$$

Each sign is comprised of two sides, or legs, and each is read from right to left. There are sixteen possible configurations for each foot, giving us a total of 256 possible odduns. In the oddun above, the right side, which is called Oché, is combined with the left side, known as Ofún, to create a compound sign Oché Ofún (usually shortened to just Oché Fun). Even though there are two sides to each oddun, the odduns are taken as a whole, and each of the 256 odduns are considered separate entities and not merely a conjunction of its two parts. The oddun above is interpreted as one entity and not merely a conjunction of Oché and Ofún, where Oché Ofún is read the same as Ofún Oché, as is the case with the diloggún divination, with sixteen possible *letras* (signs), of which only twelve can be read. If one of the other four signs appears, it means the oricha is ordering the iworo to send the person to a babalawo, as the situation requires the client to be seen with Ifá. The number of odduns in Ifá, combined with the vast amount of information associated with each oddun, expands the depth and complexity of the Ifá divination system considerably and multiplies the amount of learning necessary to become a competent babalawo. It is also common practice for babalawos to see themselves with Ifá, meaning they perform Ifá divination for themselves every day to ensure they are aligned with Ifá and the orichas, and to let them know what they can expect. This also gives the babalawo the opportunity to watch each oddun unfold in their life, giving them the insight that comes from direct experience of each individual oddun in action.

Tools of the Trade

There are two main forms of divination used by babalawos, the Table of Ifá and the ecuele (*opele* in standard Yoruba). Orunmila makes them both function by tapping into the binary system that makes up the universe and every event that will occur in it as well as in our lives.

The Table of Ifá

First and most important is the opón Ifá or Table of Ifá, which is the deepest form of divination in Ifá. It is used only for extremely important situations where deep divination is needed. Most commonly, the Table of Ifá is used to determine a person's guardian or patron oricha during initiations within Ifá and to determine an individual's personal oddun during the initial initiations into Ifá, known as *kofá* for women and *abo faca* for men. The opón, which is considered to represent the universe within its boundaries, is covered with a divination powder called *iyefá* or *iyeorosún*, on which we mark the signs as they come up.

The session opens up with a series of prayers while an *irofá* (tapper of Ifá) is tapped on the edge of the Table of Ifá to call the *egguns* (spirits of the dead), living priests, the orichas, and Orula. The irofá is usually made of deer antler or wood, but occasionally it is made of brass or ivory, and is used during prayers whenever using the Table of Ifá. Sixteen ekines are used for this form of divination. They are beaten lightly together several times, and the babalawo attempts to grab all sixteen ekin nuts at a time with his right hand. If one ekin remains in the babalawo's left hand, two lines are marked, representing zero. If two ekin nuts remain in the hand, one mark is made. If none of the ekines remain or if there are more than two remaining, the babalawo continues with the grabbing attempts until there are only one or two ekines left in his hand. This process is continued until there are eight single or double marks on the tray, making a complete oddun. Once all eight marks are made, the babalawo records the oddun, with the double lines being marked as zero and the single lines marked as one. Needless to say, this is a long and tedious process, and is one reason it is only used in situations where deep divination is required. This form of divination is used because it gives the most in-depth information on the past, present, and future, as well as answers to important questions. It is the hope that when the divination is completed, the client receives the answer to their questions and has a clear understanding of how they should proceed.

Between sessions and during breaks in the ceremonies, the ekines are kept in a calabash called a jicara and are covered with an *iruke* (a beaded horse tail switch), which is the emblem of a babalawo and can be used to cleanse a person of negativity.

The readings using the Table of Ifá are usually implemented during major initiations, and they can last several hours, with three or more babalawos giving advice to the initiate.

The Universe: The Table of Ifá

Ekines

The Ecuele

The other form of divination used by babalawos is the ecuele, which is comprised of eight disks connected to each other by a chain. The ecuele is considered the servant, or messenger, of Ifá and is the tool we use for day-to-day divination. While using the ecuele is much quicker and easier because the babalawo only needs to toss the chain to the mat once for each oddun, it is not considered as accurate as the Table of Ifá. That is why the ecuele is never used to find out a person's tutelary oricha or an individual's life oddun but is instead employed for daily matters to help a person attain balance and alignment.

The ecuele is held by the chain in the center of two sets of four disks and tossed to the mat with the connecting chain at the top. The right hand, or senior side, of the ecuele is usually marked with a set of beads so the babalawo will always be sure of which oddun has appeared.

An ecuele on the Table of Ifá

The oddun that appears on the first throw is the main oddun that accompanies the person at the time and contains the bulk of the advice

Ifá has for the client. It is the most important oddun of the consultation and the other oddums that come up, while important, serve mainly to add details to the main oddun.

From here we come to the first fork in the road and need to find out whether the oddun came *iré* (the positive side of the sign) or *osogbo* (negative side). To accomplish this, the babalawo begins by presenting a small stone to the person's forehead and asks, *"Iré ni* (does this person come with iré)?" He then hands the client the stone as well as a seashell, telling them to shake and separate them so one is in each hand. The babalawo gives the client two items to shake and hold in their hand, usually a stone and a seashell, telling them which means yes and which means no. This allows the person's own orí and her free will to enter into the equation. The babalawo then throws the ecuele twice and chooses one of the client's hands according to which oddun is senior, or higher up, in the order of the oddums. If the babalawo calls for the hand that is holding the yes object, then the person has come with iré; otherwise, the person has come with osogbo. These two oddums are considered witnesses to the primary oddun and are recorded, as they add information to the main oddun the person came with.

As each oddun has a substantial number of paths, we need to narrow them down. This is done much like the game of twenty questions, with each question requiring two oddums being cast, either with ekines or with the ecuele. The babalawo continues the questioning to find out just what kind of iré or osogbo the person came with. Most times the oddun speaks heavily of certain kinds of blessings and negativity, and these are usually the first we ask for. Continuing from there, we find out whether it is Orunmila, an oricha, or eggun who is the source of the blessing if they came in iré or will defend them in the case of osogbo. Again, most of the time the entities who figure most prominently in the oddun are asked for first.

Now we ask Ifá precisely what ebbós the client needs in order to ensure the iré will come, or what measures need to be taken to prevent any negativity associated with the sign. This can be anything from simply following Ifá's advice to offerings and even initiations that can be called for. Again, we confirm each step of the way with Ifá to make absolutely sure the work will be effective.

Finally, we ask Ifá if he is satisfied with the advice given to the client and the solutions that have been called for. If the answer is yes, then the session is officially closed. If not, we continue until Orunmila is satisfied that all that needs to be said and done has been communicated properly. During the process of an osode, it is typical for anywhere from twenty to fifty odduns to be cast.

An Actual Osode

Probably the best way to illustrate how an osode, or Ifá consultation, works is to use an actual osode as our example. In this case, we had just learned my wife was pregnant so we wanted to go to Ifá for advice and to ensure there wouldn't be any problems with the pregnancy.

As is standard, I started by giving a libation of several drops of cool water on the floor as an offering and to cool the space. Then, after saluting Olorun and Olófin, I began to salute by name the babalawos, santeros, and personal family members in my religious and blood lineages who have passed away. This act not only honors the dead, but in this way we announce our lineage to Ifá, thereby telling him who we are and where we came from. After that I continued by saluting the orichas and Orunmila himself. Finally, I told Orunmila my name in Ifá—my babalawo name—and what I was doing.

This is most often done without the babalawo knowing the reason his client has come, but in this case we both already knew. I presented the ecuele to my wife, touching her head and then certain cardinal parts of the body to ensure a strong connection is made between Ifá and her all-important orí.

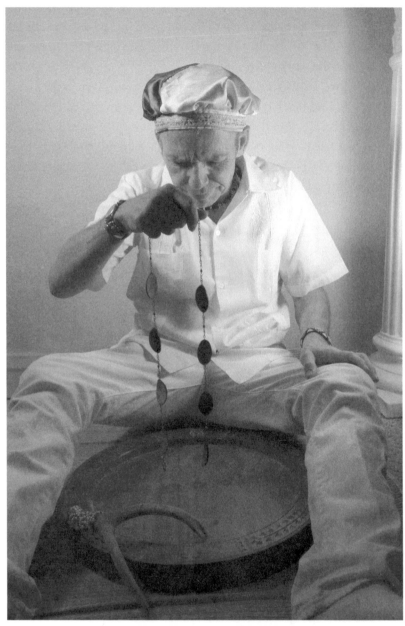

*The author performing an osode, or Ifá consultation,
using an ecuele over a Table of Ifá*

Asking for the blessings of Orunmila and any babalawos, *apetebís* (female Ifá initiates), or olorichas, I then threw the ecuele to the mat. The first oddun, called the *oddun toyale*, contains most of the advice Ifá has for the client. The oddun that appeared, and which accompanied my wife, Elizabeth, at the time, was Osaló Fobeyó. I wrote this oddun down on the paper as part of the record of the session.

Since the main oddun that came up was Osaló Fobeyó, I have to admit I was sweating bullets, because in osogbo the sign warns us that Echu is waiting at the gates of the cemetery and that emergency action would be needed. Fortunately, with the next two throws of the ecuele, I asked for her left hand that held the stone, and it was revealed to us that the sign had come with iré. Next I asked what kind of blessings could be expected, and since Ifá speaks a lot about pregnancy and children in this oddun, it seemed a pretty safe bet to ask for *iré omó* (the blessing of children). When that was confirmed, we asked if the iré was *oyale* (solid and strong), but the answer was no. We would have to work to make sure our baby would be born healthy. Finally, we asked who the iré would be coming from, and the subsequent throws of the ecuele confirmed the iré came from Orunmila himself. But Ifá had a surprise in store for us, because in the oddun Osaló Fobeyó he was telling us we would be having *ibeyis* (twins)! The doctor confirmed this soon afterward.

Ifá went on to inform us that Obatalá would mark one of the children, claiming the child as his own, and that we should expect the twins to be as different as night and day, as illustrated by a parable for the oddun where two complete opposites sat at the same table. In our case, we soon found out that we were being blessed with a boy and a girl, so even their genders were opposites, and we soon learned that their personalities would also be as different as night and day.

Knowing that the iré in this case was coming from Orunmila, we asked him what we needed to do in order to ensure the pregnancy would come to term and the babies would be born healthy. As it turned out, the babies needed to go through the highly unusual step of performing the first part of the ceremonies for their initial initiation in Ifá, even though they would still be in their mother's womb at the time! Of course, we immediately began to make the necessary preparations to have this done.

Both children were born healthy, even though there were a few scares along the way, as was predicted by Ifá. Within minutes after the birth, our son, Emiliano, rolled over to reveal a huge mole on his lower back. So here was Obatalá's child, as predicted by Ifá. When we completed the ceremonies for their kofá and abo faca a few months after their birth and determined who their orichas were, we confirmed Emiliano was indeed a child of Obatalá and that our daughter, Xochitl, turned out to be a child of Changó. As they grew a little older, we soon found their personalities couldn't possibly be more opposite, once again confirming the old saying in Ifá, "*La palabra de Orula nunca cae al piso* (the word of Orula never falls to the floor)."

This example illustrates how some Ifá predictions can take months or even years to come to pass. It can take years to fully see the depth of what Ifá reveals, even if you're a babalawo.

Now that we have seen how a typical session occurs, let's break it down into the different parts. Each part of the session has a specific purpose in revealing the client's situation and assuring them the most fulfilling outcome. This is largely achieved through a series of yes or no questions that we ask Ifá.

Babalawo divining with the Table of Ifá

The Oddun Toyale

This is the actual oddun out of the 256 possible that accompanies the person during a divination session, or osode. This oddun is the focus of the session, and the babalawo will recite from the wealth of advice, patakís, refránes, and remedies, or ebbós, that apply to the oddun that comes up for the person.

The Testigos, or Witnesses

These are the first two signs that are thrown after the initial oddun toyale has been acquired. The two signs are the first splits in the road where we find whether the orientation of the sign is in iré or osogbo. The two witnessing signs are also marked down by the babalawo and discussed, as Ifá is speaking to the client through those signs as well. We should understand that having a sign come with iré doesn't necessarily guarantee that good will come or that the negative aspects of the sign won't come to pass. On the other hand, if we come with osogbo, the sign can be turned to iré or at least have the negative impact vastly lessened. The fact is you can turn the iré into osogbo or vice versa. It all depends on how well you follow Orula's advice and prescriptions.

One should always remember that iré is always more fragile and takes more work to retain than osogbo. This dates back to ancient times when the irés and osogbos were all kings who went to Orula to be seen with Ifá. They were advised to make an ebbó to avoid losing their positions. The irés, including health, money, wives, or children, refused to make the ebbó, as they considered themselves superior because everybody was always happy to see them and they were welcomed all over the world. Only the osogbos made the required offering. Not long after, all the irés threw a party for themselves and didn't invite the osogbos, whom they considered inferior to them. Echu then sent a beautiful gift with a letter that simply said, "To the most beautiful wife of all the irés." It didn't take long for all the wives to start arguing about who was the most beautiful, and soon the irés themselves got pulled into the argument. The disagreement worsened, and all the irés killed each other in the fight that ensued.

From that day forward, the osogbos—death, sickness, and loss—have always been more permanent and forceful than the irés.

The Nature of the Iré or Osogbo

As mentioned above, after we have arrived at the witnessing signs we ask a number of questions using the ecuele or the ekines to pinpoint the details of the iré or osogbo. What kind of iré is it? Is it *iré aikú* (health), iré omó, or *iré lalafia* (general well-being)? If the sign comes in osogbo, is it *osogbo ikú* (death), *arun* (sickness), *ofo* (loss), or something else? And if the person has come in iré, at whose feet will it be found? Is it *elese eggun* (at the feet of the dead); the oricha Orunmila; or does it come from Olófin or *eledá* (the person's own head)? If the person comes in osogbo, which one of these forces is willing to defend the person and help them to get back that state of balance and alignment known as iré?

Ifá Says

Once we have pinpointed the particular path of the oddun, we are in a position to interpret the advice Ifá has for the person. At this point we will tell the person the relevant proverbs, advice, and any warnings Ifá may have that apply to that particular path of the oddun. Often we will tell patakís that illustrate how the oddun typically unfolds in a person's life.

Ebbó

From here, we investigate what Ifá says we need to do to put the person back in alignment. This can be anything from simply following Orunmila's advice to various offerings, a *keborí eledá* (also known as a *rogación de la cabeza* in Spanish) to cleanse and strengthen the head, or an *ebbó katero* (a complex ritual using the Table of Ifá), an initiation, or even receiving an oricha or a *paraldo* (an intense ceremony to remove an unhealthy spirit plaguing a person).

I have found that for many people the most difficult ebbó is simply following Orunmila's advice. Sometimes Orunmila will not ask for any offerings but instead will tell the person how they must change in order to live a more fulfilled life. This is because the imbalance and lack of alignment the person is experiencing is due to their own actions and way of being, which cannot be solved for long by any offering or cleansing. Many times it is an imbalance in one of the person's greatest strengths that is causing the problems. This is because all strengths and virtues are double-edged swords with their inherent weaknesses and problems.

One example would be the case where a person's greatest asset is their strength of will. When that strength of will gets out of balance, it becomes simple stubbornness and tyranny that may cause the person untold problems, not only in their relationships and any aspect of life that deals with other people, but also in the failure to see that anyone or anything might be seeing a side of things that they might be missing. Another case would be a person who by nature is patient and weighs all factors before making decisions. While their judgment may be impeccable, that strength becomes a weakness and a problem when that person finds themselves incapable of making decisions while waiting for more information. Thus, nothing is ever decided by them and is often decided for them by circumstances, many times to their detriment. People may be spending all of their time undoing themselves because it is the person's own behavior and way of thinking that is working against their well-being.

To make changes to one's own life may be the most difficult thing of all to accomplish, and most people don't relish that sort of effort and would much prefer to have some sort of exotic ceremony performed on them to take care of their problems for them. Little do they know that making changes in themselves can be strong medicine and can have a powerful effect on their own well-being and success in life.

Remember, the purpose of Ifá divination is designed to put you in balance and alignment with your own destiny so you won't be told to do anything against your true nature. If a person is strong-willed by nature, they will not be told to become meek, self-effacing, and subservient. They may be told they have to learn that they are not made weak by listening and following the advice of others. If a person is passionate and adventurous by nature, they will not be told to become emotionless and timid. They may be told they must not let their passions run away with them to the point that they become self-destructive. In this way, changing our own behavior becomes a powerful ebbó in and of itself.

"That Doesn't Apply to Me!"

Sometimes it seems that the advice Orunmila is giving doesn't appear to apply to the situation the person is consulting about. This usually occurs for one of two reasons:

1. The events simply have not happened yet. In this situation I often get what I refer to as The Call. A few days or weeks later, the person will call and tell me the things Ifá had warned about has come to pass, much to the person's surprise. For example, Ifá has warned more than one client of mine that a woman could come into their life and threaten their marriage. In one case, the client openly laughed at me. A few weeks later, his wife came home early to find some rather intimate correspondence from another woman left up on his computer screen, and needless to say, he wasn't laughing at Ifá anymore.

2. Sometimes the real cause of a person's problems is not always obvious. For example, a person might be rushed to the hospital with a life-threatening case of blood poisoning only to find out the blood poisoning was caused by an abscessed tooth, which could have been easily prevented if acted upon early enough.

Itá

"We are as Obatalá made us, but what we are to become we make ourselves."

When we are born, unfortunately we do not come with an owner's manual to help us best find fulfillment in our lives. Thus, we may end up spending our lives undoing ourselves and working against our own best interests and our true destiny in life. Perhaps if we had an owner's manual, we could avoid many of the pitfalls we succumb to every day, and know what we need to do to ensure a fulfilling and successful life.

The *itá* (deep divination) received during the kofá and abo faca initiations are that owner's manual. The kofá and abo faca are the fundamental initiations into Ifá for women and men. During this three-day ceremony, they are not only placed under the protection and blessings of Orula but receive an itá that will guide them throughout their lives.

Using the Table of Ifá, the babalawos painstakingly bring down the oddun that will accompany the initiate for life and that has accompanied them since birth. During the itá, one by one the babalawos present tell you about the oddun that accompanies you, and the advice that Orula gives you on how to best fulfill your destiny. You are told the things to watch out for, the things to avoid, and the things you should do to better your life. You will often be told things that you will realize have been ongoing and repeating patterns that have always been with you. Other things are brought up that speak of events you can expect in your future.

During the itá, it is not uncommon for you to receive certain *ewós* (prohibitions) that are part of the oddun that you came with. Those ewós are there for your own good. For example, I have a godchild who was told she was prohibited from eating pork, something she complained bitterly about, as pork was her favorite food. A few days later, she recalled having had to go to the hospital on three separate occasions, each time after having eaten bad pork!

During the deep divination of the itá you receive when you are initiated into Ifá, you receive an oddun that has accompanied you since you were born and will be with you for your entire life. In this case, any or all paths of the sign can apply to you at one point or another, so it is very important to familiarize yourself with all the paths of your particular oddun. The oddun one receives during the itá for the kofá or abo faca initiation is your destiny and can only be superseded if one is later initiated as a babalawo or as an apetebí ayafá. Itás received during other initiations are for life as well and complement the itá given during kofá and abo faca.

Another difference between the itá and a regular divination is that since the sign is for life in an itá, any iré or osogbo that comes with the oddun is not necessarily permanent. For example, if your oddun in life comes in osogbo, it is more of a warning because that osogbo can be changed into iré if you complete all the ebbós called for and closely follow the advice given in the itá. On the other hand, you can come with the most beautiful iré during your itá and through your own actions or inaction that iré can be turned into the osogbo side of your oddun.

Sometimes when there is no way to completely avoid an event from happening, there are tricks we can use. For instance, if we find that it is inevitable a person will go to the hospital, we might advise the client to find a way to get put in a hospital room or bed for a time. This can sometimes be done if you have a friend or acquaintance who works in a hospital who can find an empty room for you for a few minutes.

There are myriad tactics and recipes such as this that can be used to avoid the pitfalls and ensure the good that each oddun predicts. Sometimes a person can become particularly proficient at navigating their oddun, achieving all the good while avoiding the negative side. We say of such a person, "She knows how to live her sign."

Chapter Three
Babalawo

In a land called Sukanilé, which was part of the Iyesa nation, there was an obá who was a true seeker of the mysteries of life as well as a great thinker. At one point, he brought together the wisest people in his kingdom and asked them to show him the true nature of the world. They held a number of great councils where they finally came to the agreement that reality simply could not be defined, then went before the obá to tell him their conclusion. This only made the king all the more determined to find out the truth, and he began to travel throughout his kingdom in hopes of finding someone who could enlighten him about the true nature of the world.

Meanwhile, along the borderlands of Iyesaland there lived a babalawo named Ifá Kandashé. He was well known in his area for his outstanding interpretations of Ifá's odduns, but because he lived out in the boondocks, he was forced to live off of decorating statues, vases, and pots.

He was getting bored with it, and as he never received visits from any of the great people he would hear about, he set about making ebbó with a pot, the paints, and the tools of his trade. While he was asleep, a drunken Changó came by and painted lightning bolts. Eleggúa, who had just finished eating a young rooster, came by next and put his bloody hands all over the cazuela. Finally, the great artist Ere Oyola, the Rainbow Serpent who represented Olodumare, took his turn and defecated into the vase. By the time the orichas were through, the pot was truly a mess.

All this time, Ifá Kandashé managed to sleep through the entire thing. When he woke up and saw the mess painted in his pot, he exclaimed, "Orunmila be praised! But what—what is this thing?"

At the same moment, a grand procession appeared at his home, and royal messengers knock on his door. When he bid them to enter, he suddenly realized it was the obá himself. The king of the entire nation was in his house, along with an entourage of wise men from throughout the land! Shocked, the babalawo Kandashé asked them what they wished.

The obá responded, "You are Ifá Kandashé, as famous in my land as you are in your own for interpreting Ifá odduns better than anyone else. I wish to know something that all my wise advisors haven't been able to show me."

"What is that?" asked the perplexed babalawo.

"That you show me the true nature of the world," the obá responded.

Ifá Kandashé, after analyzing everything the king had told him, finally said, "Look inside this pot and you will see the world as it really is!"

The obá eagerly grabbed the pot and looked inside … and looked … and looked. Finally, the king broke into paroxysms of laughter and exclaimed, "You are so right! You are truly, truly wise! In reality, the world is nothing but randomness and shit! From this day forward, you shall be my head diviner and the counselor of my court, and you shall always be showered with treasures and honors!"

---

*"To study Ifá without thinking about it is in vain;
to think about Ifá without studying it is dangerous."*

"Wisdom is the most refined beauty a babalawo can possess."

"Ifá can save you," said the babalawo who was to become my *oyugbona* (assistant padrino) for the initiation.

"What the hell do you mean by that?" my padrino in Ifá, Pete, shot back in his inimitable direct manner.

"He has to make his Ifá to become a babalawo."

These were the opening words of the itá for my abo faca initiation, the divination telling me my itá in life. I was to be initiated into the priesthood of Ifá, the oricha of wisdom and diviner for humanity, the orichas, and Olodumare (God) himself. Specializing in divination, the rituals and offerings associated with it, the babalawo is also the caretaker of the oral traditions of the religion, the secrets of the oricha, the secrets of life … and the universe. My childhood wish was being answered.

Babalawo

In her impressive work *The Anagó Language of Cuba*, obá oriaté and scholar Maria Concordia (Oggún Gbemi) defines the babalawo as "an eternal student of Ifá and representation of its earthly manifestation, who must know everything regarding the rituals and ceremonies, divinatory advices, prayers, chants, and sacrifices related to the philosophy and theology of Lucumí religion." [1]

Besides being the living repositories of the sum total of our oral traditions and ritual knowledge, the babalawos act as the exclusive interpreters of Ifá's divine messages for the community as well as for individuals. Therefore, as the refrán above tells us, babalawos must dedicate themselves to the constant expansion and deepening of their knowledge, and Orula enjoins us to study and contemplate Ifá so babalawos may know and understand Ifá.

A babalawo is expected to follow a strict code of conduct. He should be honest, simple, and of unassailable character, serving as an inspiration to those around him. He should constantly maintain only the highest ethical standards and must endlessly strive to be worthy of only the greatest respect. As my oyugbona Julito said so many years ago, "You don't make Ifá for power or for money. You make Ifá so Orula can save you."

The babalawo always has the history of Obí's vanity to remind him of the price to be paid for becoming too proud and arrogant.

Obí Agbón (coconut) was very humble and honest, so Olófin dressed him in white inside and out, and placed him in a very high position as one of Olófin's principal diviners.

But over time, Obí became arrogant and overly proud of his position.

One day he threw a party in his palace and invited all the crème de la crème of society and Elegguá. Having noticed the changes in Obí's character, Eleggúa brought all the homeless and the beggars he could find from the marketplace.

Obí took Eleggúa aside, telling him, "I invited you, but not all of these people."

Eleggúa looked Obí in the eye and replied, "If they go, I go," and stomped out.

A few weeks later Olófin asked Eleggúa to deliver a message to Obí, but Eleggúa said, "You know I would do anything for you, but please send someone else to go to Obí's palace."

"Why don't you want to go?" asked Olófin.

With this, Eleggúa told Olófin about what had occurred at Obí's party. What Eleggúa didn't know is that he was merely confirming what Olófin already knew.

So Olófin dressed like the filthiest of the homeless and went to Obí's palace. When Obí saw the beggar at his door, he slammed the door right in his face!

Suddenly, the walls shook as Olófin's voice thundered, "Obí ti o fe ni (don't you recognize who I am)?"

With that, Obí prostrated himself before Olófin and begged forgiveness. But Olófin cursed him to always be dark on the outside and white only on the inside to show the world the price of arrogance. He would fall from the trees to always remind him of his fall from great heights due to his pride. People would slap him and kick him once he was on the ground. And to remind the world of his duplicity, he would always have two faces, one light and one dark. And lastly, he would still divine; however, he would never have a voice of his own but could only speak for others.

Not everyone is born to be a babalawo or an obá oriaté or a santera or santero, for that matter. Traditionally in Cuba, it wasn't commonplace for a person to become an iworo, and it was downright rare to become a babalawo. It meant years of work and then more years of saving up the money for the initiation. It was always meant to be a sacrifice—not a commodity to be bought by spiritual tourists collecting initiations—if you were chosen to become a priest by the orichas in the first place. If a person is meant to become a babalawo, it will usually come up while they are being seen with Ifá and must be confirmed when they receive their abo faca. For me, finding out that Ifá had chosen me to be one of his priests came the very first time I was seen with Ifá, but the prognostication had to be confirmed when I received my abo faca.

One of the babalawos working in that abo faca ceremony was to become my assistant padrino for this initiation. His name was Julito Collazo (Iwori Kosó ibae), whom I would later learn was not only a famous babalawo but a famous drummer as well. Julito Collazo and Francisco Aguabella were the first and best religious drummers in the country and were, along with the babalawo Pancho Mora, among the first practicing priests in the United States. Padrino Julito was also a famous secular drummer, often playing with other greats such as Tito Puente, Celia Cruz, and Mongo Santamaria. During a break in the ceremonies, Julito came over and began casually talking about Ifá and the religion in general. Suddenly he became very serious and looked me directly in the eyes.

"I'm going to tell you something very important. You don't make Ifá for power. You don't make Ifá for money. You make Ifá so Orula can save you." With those words, he turned and strode back into the igbodún to continue the work of consecrating the first kofás and abo facas to be received in San Francisco.

On the third day, the day of the itá, where Ifá reveals our destinies through deep divination using the Table of Ifá, I went into the initiation room to learn my path in life. After they had gotten my oddun in abo faca and its orientation, it was time to speak about my sign and what it meant.

"Ifá can save you." With those few words, padrino Julito had informed that it was indeed my destiny to become a babalawo.

But having the odduns to make Ifá (become initiated as a babalawo) is just the beginning. There are a number of prohibitions that can prevent a person from being initiated as an Ifá priest. If a person has ever been *ridden* (possessed) by an oricha or an *eggun* (the dead), they are not allowed to go on to Ifá. The vast majority of babalawos are *oluwos*, babalawos who have been initiated as an iworo before going on to become an Ifá priest. But if they initiate another person, they are discouraged from becoming a babalawo, as they would not be able to fulfill many of their responsibilities to the orichas and to their godchildren. And if they are an initiated santero, they must first receive permission from their oricha before they can become a babalawo. My own padrino, as an oricha priest, Guillermo Diago Obá Bí, was denied initiation as a priest of Ifá in this way. He had the odduns to make Ifá, but Changó would not allow him to become a babalawo. His destiny was to become a truly great obá oriaté, and he was a real treasure in his own right.

Because I made *Obatalá* (was initiated as a priest of Obatalá) before making Ifá, I still needed the obá oriaté to ask Obatalá for his permission and blessing before I could pass to Ifá. Not only did I get his permission, but also five years later when I made Ifá, Obatalá spoke up, giving me his iré, Maferefún Obatalá, which means we always give thanks to Obatalá.

I have my Padrino Pete Rivera to thank for making sure no phases were skipped and everything was well done every step of the way. Padrino Pete has always been like a second father to me, and I am forever in his debt. He has always led me in the right direction and has been a model godparent to me.

Many of these prohibitions are in place because Orula demands that his priests devote themselves exclusively to Ifá, one cannot be a part-time babalawo. In fact, this demand for complete devotion to Ifá is dramatically and sometimes painfully illustrated during the ceremony called the *iyoyé*, as we shall see.

This brings us to the most controversial prohibition in Ifá, which is the prohibition against initiating women as Ifá priests. For the initiation of a babalawo to be valid, the presence of *Igba Odun* (the calabash of Odun) in the igbodún or Ifá initiation shrine is absolutely necessary. Odun is the ultimate source of Ifá's power and those who have received her make up the highest rank among the babalawos. And because Olófin/Odun is the source of all odduns giving us the power to know their secrets and to work with them, to be initiated without her doesn't make any sense. That is why the oddun Oché Yekú states directly that a person initiated as an Ifá priest without Odun has accomplished nothing and will not be recognized by Ifá.

As we will see in the next chapter, Odun, also known as Olófin, is so crucial to the initiation of an Ifá priest that in the late 1800s, a babalawo named Adechina risked his life to go back to Africa and bring Olófin/ Odun back to the island so babalawos could be initiated in Cuba. Olófin's presence was crucial enough for our greatest ancestor to risk life and limb to bring Olófin back to Cuba; and instead of staying in Africa, he left his home a second time so Ifá could survive there. After the immense sacrifices made on the part of Lucumí Ifá's greatest ancestor, the idea of initiating an Ifá priest without Olófin is unconceivable for us. These are the Lucumí babalawo's roots and we simply won't betray them for anyone, no matter what the prevailing attitudes may be at the time. Our traditions did not survive the ordeals of slavery only to die in a hot tub in Esalen. Olófin/Odun does not permit women to be in her presence, which will be discussed later, and that is why babalawos are not allowed to initiate women as Ifá priests.

There is the elegán initiation for men seen in some parts of Africa, but we don't recognize that initiation because Odun is not present during their initiation. In fact, in many of the areas of Yorubaland that has the elegán initiation, the elegán is only allowed to divine for himself and his immediate family using the ecuele, and is not allowed to divine using the ekin nuts or initiate others into Ifá, because they are not considered full-fledged Ifá priests.

Initiation

The Afro-Cuban babalawos must be fully initiated as Ifá priests in the ceremony called atefá before they can begin to learn the secrets of the odduns, which may or may not be the case in different parts of Yorubaland.[2] The initiation of a babalawo lasts seven days, during which the new initiate is secluded in the igbodún, which means "Odun's Forest." The room gets this name, because although the person becomes a priest of Orula, it is Orula's wife Odun's presence that ultimately gives the new initiate the aché to interpret and work with the odduns of Ifá.

Early during the initiation, the new initiate divines with Ifá for his first time and the oddun that appears is their sign for life. A babalawo's entire life from birth to death is contained in that oddun. From then on, other Ifá priests know a babalawo by this oddun, and babalawos usually refer to each other by their oddun. For instance, my sign is Baba Eyiogbe, so I'm known as Frank Baba Eyiogbe, Baba Eyiogbe, or Eyiogbe. Babalawos know a great deal about each other as soon as they are introduced.

The Iyoyé

"The roots of Ifá are bitter, but the fruits are sweet."

The air of anticipation is palpable among the small crowd of onlookers waiting for the new initiate to appear in the doorway to the igbodún. It has been a week since he was sequestered into the room for continuous ceremonies, sacrifices, cleansings, and intensive learning and is now making his first re-appearance into the world. What is about to take place is the most dramatic of the closing ceremonies and the only ceremony non-initiates are allowed to witness.

The new initiate steps out into the morning. He is shirtless and barefoot, his pants rolled up above his knees. Over his shoulder he carries a hoe and a machete as he makes his way toward a small makeshift farm laid out on the patio. The farm is tiny, only needing to be large enough to relive the history from unspeakably ancient times in the life of the ancient initiate Akalá, imbuing the ritual with the power of those primordial events. On either side of his path to the farm stands a row of his babalawo brethren armed with *cujes*, long, thin branches that seem designed to cut through skin as sharply as they cut through the air. Cut from a special bush known for its healing qualities called *rasca barriga* (belly scraper), the cujes are used to ensure the future health of the new babalawo. You can hear the whistle of the sticks as the babalawos make practice strikes to test the strength of their weapons and the nerve of the new babalawo. The *awó* (anyone initiated as an Ifá priest) is now led out of the igbodún by his oyugbona, armed with a cuje of his own to defend his apprentice from the worst of the blows to come, and they walk toward the farm to plant the first seedlings.

"Akalá omo oricha, Akalá omo oricha, Orunmila mabinu, Akalá omo oricha," the *Orbá Oriaté* or Master of Ceremonies, intones *"Akalá child of*

the oricha, Akalá child of the oricha, Orunmila, please don't be angry, Akalá child of the oricha." All the babalawos repeat back the song in the call and response, hinting at the meaning of the ceremony.

On the way back toward the room from planting his crops, the sticks come whistling down, raining sharp wooden pain onto the back and legs of the new babalawo. As much as his oyugbona tries to block the sticks, the blows are fast and coming from too many directions. Many find their mark slicing through air and skin with equal agility. The oyugbona and the determined young farmer then make their way back to the Ifá room. Once at the igbodún, they get a brief moment of reprieve from the onslaught as they prepare to head back out to the farm and the gauntlet of waiting babalawos and their cujes.

They must pass through the gauntlet seven times in each direction and the burning pain becomes stronger and more cutting, the new babalawo's back now crisscrossed with stripes left by the cujes. Finally he is allowed to return to the initiation room to kneel before his Oluwo Siwayú, who is the babalawo who initiated him to Ifá, and gives him his blessing and soothes him by applying a liquid to his stinging back. The pain will pass within a few weeks, but the initiate is now a Father of the Secrets for life. The babalawos who just moments before were giving the new initiate the beating of his life now file into the room to congratulate the newest member of their ranks, who, in the realm of spiritual warriors, has just become the spiritual equivalent of a Navy SEAL. With that, the new babalawo goes on to enjoy his first ceremonial dinner with his fellow babalawos and to start the truly hard work that is ahead of him. Within hours, this room—that had been magically transformed for a week into the primordial grove where babalawos have been initiated since time immemorial—will be closed, sealed, and become just an ordinary room again.

Although at first blush it might seem this is little more than a testosterone-fueled hazing with a spiritual justification, that is the furthest thing from the truth. The iyoyé is actually the re-enactment of an event from ancient times when a babalawo was initiated to Ifá. During his initiation, he was warned that he must work Ifá exclusively, but he decided that being a farmer would be easier and more profitable. Because he was denying his true destiny, it was not long before his suffering began, which is represented by being beaten with the cujes. Finally, the babalawo returned to Ifá, where his pain and suffering ceased and he began to prosper spiritually and materially.

The babalawos are the only priests within the Lucumí religion who are made to swear before Orunmila and Olófin/Odun to help humanity during their initiation. The Ifá priests are not only expected to help all people who come to them for help without judging them, but they are expected to work for the good of the entire world. Every babalawo is made to swear to protect the secrets of Ifá as well. There is a case that is famous among Havana babalawos where a babalawo decided to renounce the religion and, in the process, revealed some of Ifá's secrets to an ethnologist. Afterward, when the babalawo became extremely ill, he went to a babalawo, where it came up that he had to go through the iyoyé ceremony all over again to save his life. To show the world what happens to people who reveal Ifa's secrets, the babalawos videotaped the ceremony, which, due to the man's offense, was extremely severe. But Orula cured the babalawo of his illness, and he returned to Ifá and never revealed any secrets again.

Training

Being initiated as an Ifá priest is just the beginning, and it is only *after* being initiated that the training begins in earnest. The teaching of a competent babalawo typically takes three to five years.

The preparation of a babalawo begins during the initiation week, and my initiation in Havana, Cuba, was no exception. In my case, the teaching during my week on the throne was intense, to put it mildly. Every morning around three o'clock, my oyugbona would shove me with his foot so we could begin my training for the day. He would shake me awake, ecuele in hand, which he would arrange to produce different odduns that I would groggily attempt to identify in the semi-dark.

Like every Afro-Cuban babalawo, on the first day as an Ifá priest I learned to say, *"awo chudú; awo didé,"* (which means "a babalawo falls; another babalawo lifts them up") any time I dropped an ekin during divination with the Table of Ifá. To dramatize this, the babalawo is taught to pick up the fallen ekin while holding another ekin in their hand. With this act, the Ifá priest is given a lesson on how a babalawo should always give aid to another member of their fraternity in need. And this lesson is pounded in every single time a babalawo divines with their ekin because no divination session with the ekines finishes without some of the ekines falling. And the great babalawos who became legends, such as Adechina and Tata Gaitán, took that lesson further, extending those lessons and the attitude to all of humanity and the world.

One afternoon during my week in seclusion, Padrino Miguelito came into the room with an entourage of about six or seven elder babalawos and handed me a two-page-long *moyuba*, which is a lengthy prayer used at the beginning of virtually every ritual. He recited it to me slowly and clearly so I could hear the correct pronunciation of the words, and then informed me I would be tested on it the next morning. With that, they all shuffled out of the room. The next morning, sure enough, all the babalawos returned, and I was asked to recite the moyuba. Although I was extremely nervous trying to recite the prayer in front of so many elders, I managed to focus and get through the whole prayer. As I neared the end of the prayer, Padrino Miguelito began to chuckle, sharing a knowing look with the other babalawos, who were also amused for some reason. At the end, Padrino Miguelito merely shrugged and said, *"Asi es Baba Eyiogbe,"* meaning "That's Baba Eyiogbe." At that, all the babalawos broke into laughter. Only then did I realize that not every new babalawo was expected to memorize the whole prayer in one evening. I had been up all night, pacing and reciting the passages, gradually adding to them little by little until I finally had the whole prayer memorized. When they all shuffled out, laughing and joking amongst themselves, I was exhausted but happy that I had passed the test. I also found out that day although a lot is expected of every new babalawo, even more is expected if you are the child of certain signs.

I knew then I had a lot of hard work ahead of me. There are 256 odduns, each one having its own secrets, prayers, histories, proverbs, ebbós, plants, *iches* (works), and even its own path of Echu. When I reached the end of the information I was given on the odduns, I had to laugh at Ifá's humor. The very last oddun started off by saying that a babalawo cannot know everything, and only Orula and Olófin will ever know it all. Like most babalawos, I was taught to see myself with Ifá every morning. Not only is that a good way to know what to expect that day, but it is also a marvelous opportunity to learn a new oddun every day in greater depth.

Ifá is an oral tradition passed down from padrino to *ahijado* (godchild) and from listening carefully to elders. There are also a number of books and papers on Ifá that have become available since the 1940s, a few of them are good but most of them are poor. Many are filled with what my padrino Miguelito in Cuba calls *inventos de papeles* (fraudulent inventions coming from papers), and particularly bad ones are crammed with *sancochos* (pig slop). Sometimes I even have to wonder if some of these books and papers are intentionally incomplete and filled with errors to fool non-babalawos and those babalawos who haven't bothered to learn from their godparents. The books in English are often even worse, sometimes to the point of being unintentionally funny. For instance, there was one book, an English translation of Spanish texts selling for more than $700, which had mistaken the word *anguila* (eel) for *aguila* (eagle), going on to advise the reader to put this eagle into a container of water until it dies. Not even talking about the ethical and legal issues surrounding the killing of an endangered species, one can imagine the kinds of wounds the unhappy babalawo would suffer while trying to drown an eagle in a bucket of water!

That's not to say there aren't any good books on Ifá out there. For instance, there is *Iwe ni Iyewó ni Ifá Orunmila,* published in the 1940s. Although Pedro Arango was listed as the author, he is more likely to be the compiler rather than the actual author.[3] Pedro Arango turns out to be quite a mystery, a kind of Lucumí version of B. Traven. First, Arango was a child of Oggún and would have been prohibited from being initiated as a babalawo. Since he was not a babalawo, how did he come to know so much about Ifá's odduns? As Emma Teran (Ochún Yemí) had initiated him to Oggún in the 1950s, Arango apparently wasn't even an oloricha when he wrote the book. Further, Emma Teran asserted that Pedro Arango did not know how to read or write and was thus incapable of having written any books, much less a detailed book on Ifá odduns. It is thought that the extremely knowledgeable and powerful babalawo Miguel Febles (Odí Ka) was among the babalawos who were the actual sources of the book, and Tata Gaitán has also been mentioned as a possible source.

These books were extremely restricted and were manually typed out one by one, as copy machines did not exist. In a preface to the second edition of *Iwe ni Iyewó ni Ifá Orunmila*, Arango complains that three copies of the first edition fell into the hands of a woman, presumably an oloricha, and two oriatés. Needless to say, the babalawos were outraged that these books, which were intended for the exclusive use of Ifá priests, had fallen into the hands of a few unscrupulous santeros. To ensure no more copies of the book would fall into the hands of non-babalawos, Arango further claimed to have taken new measures. To identify anyone who attempted to share the book with non-babalawos, not only did he record the address of each person buying the book, but each copy also had a secret mark to identify the individual copy. Arango then added that anyone caught sharing the book with non-babalawos would be denounced publicly to their elders.[4, 5]

At one juncture, Ramon Febles (Ogbe Tuanilara), Bernardo Rojas (Irete Untedí), and Pablo "El Periquito" Pérez (Ogbe Yono), after realizing the necessity of preserving the knowledge of the surviving African-born elders such as Ño José Akonkón (Oyekun Meyi) and Adechina (Obara Meyi), took an unprecedented course of action. To ensure the knowledge of these elders would not be lost, they began to record their teachings. Apparently all the elders they approached were agreeable to this, except for Ño Akonkón. While he was more than willing to teach, he would not allow anyone to take notes, believing that everything should be learned by memorization alone. Ramon Febles, who housed, clothed, and fed Ño Akonkón, in the tradition of washing the feet of elders, arranged for the three of them to visit the elder babalawo. While two of them would get Ño Akonkón to talk about Ifá and the odduns, the third would hide outside an open window frantically scribbling down everything he said.

Evidently these notes were eventually published in Havana under the title *Tratado de Odduns de Ifá* (Treatise on the Ifá's Odduns), and it is likely the oldest Ifá document in existence. Put together so babalawos would have access to a massive amount of knowledge of Ifá in one place, it is obvious that this book was taken from notes, and some who are not grounded in knowledge of the odduns may find it difficult to understand.[6] Since the books presumed the babalawo would know certain aspects of the rituals, some steps are often not included. These omissions also made it difficult for the uninitiated to put together and perform these rituals correctly. Since the publishing of this original tome, there have been a number of books by this name released. Some of these books were copies of the original with numerous typographical errors and additions mixed in, and others bore no resemblance to the original whatsoever. Needless to say, this has created a lot of confusion.

There is a third book I received through my padrino that I found extremely useful, but being that it is a copy of a copy, I have no idea if it was once published or simply an extremely detailed *libreta* (notebook) containing information on all the odduns.

History

Ogbe Di Kaka Ogbe Di Lele: The Learning Never Stops

In the oddun Ogbe Di there is a parable that tells us how Orunmila traveled all over the world seeking knowledge. This patakí speaks directly to babalawos, informing us that the knowledge of Ifá is not all in one place and never can be. Knowledge of Ifá is to be shared among babalawos wherever they might be:

> Orula, the wisest person on earth, had been placed in charge of doling out his wisdom to the world. While on earth he taught the art and science of Ifá, but he held back some of his knowledge because he feared some of the babalawos might prove to be unworthy.
>
> Olófin decided Orula had been on earth long enough to complete his mission, but soon found out that he had held back some of his wisdom and had not taught everything.
>
> Olófin was not satisfied and sent Orula back to earth to finish his mission, accompanied by Echu Elegguá who convened an Ifá assembly with all the babalawos on earth. As each babalawo talked about an od-

*dun, Ogbe Di would add to their knowledge until all of his knowledge
had been shared with the world. No one knows for sure whether it was
Echu's idea or Orula's, but there was just one catch: no one babalawo received all the knowledge. Instead, each babalawo received a piece of it.*

*When Orula had finished teaching, Elegguá told him, "There is
only one piece of knowledge you lack. Your time has come to leave this
world."*

*And with that, Ogbe Di was taken to the Other World to be with
Olófin. And all the knowledge is indeed on earth, but each babalawo
only has a piece of it. And that way babalawos must seek each other
out, wherever they may be. In this manner, the fraternity of babalawos
is strengthened as well as the wisdom and knowledge of Ifá in general.*

Just as Orula himself traveled the ends of the earth seeking knowledge,
the babalawo must seek knowledge of Ifá wherever it may be found,
whether it is Cuba or Africa. This oddun explains the natural tendency
among babalawos to eagerly seek out knowledge from one another,
deepening and strengthening their own knowledge and the wisdom of
Ifá in general. Oshitola, an African babalawo from Ibadan in Yorubal-
and, exemplifies this trait when he informs us that if a Cuban babalawo
came to him with advice about his oddun, he would need to follow the
words of wisdom.

In my own oddun, Baba Eyiogbe, there is a short but profound parable that comes from Africa and is often told by babalawos from there:

*Orunmila was initiated, but instead of resting on his laurels he plunged
himself right back into the forest where he had been initiated in order to
re-initiate himself anew.*

The parable ends with the refrán, "If you reach the top of the palm
tree, you should not let go." In other words, even if you somehow manage to become the greatest babalawo in the world, you would still need
to keep striving to keep from falling from your lofty position. No matter
how much we know, we must keep learning as a perpetual beginner, always striving to learn and to know more. These parables illustrate how a

babalawo's training and learning never stops, and I often joke about how people will know for sure when I have stopped learning—they will see me being lowered into a six-by-six foot hole.

Although they are indeed initiated, tradition dictates that babalawos are not permitted to practice Ifá until they have accumulated enough knowledge and experience to receive formal permission from their Oluwo Siguayú (padrino) to begin working as a babalawo. Flying down to Cuba or Nigeria and paying a few thousand dollars to get initiated does not make you a babalawo. In my case, I received this *licencia* (formal permission) twice. Once from my Padrino Pete, and again later from Padrino Miguelito, who had directed my initiation into Ifá and was my padrino for the initiations I received after Padrino Pete became too ill to work Ifá. I still remember the day my padrino finally told me *"Ya estas listo* (you are ready)."* and gave me his formal permission to work as a babalawo.

Chapter Four
Ifá Comes to Cuba

There was once a prince who had been exiled in disgrace from his father's kingdom. Destitute and desperate, he went for Ifá divination to find a solution to his woes. Ifá told the young prince that he must offer sacrifice by going into the forest to burn his last remaining possessions, which were the very clothes off his back. Only through this final loss would he come to achieve the great destiny that awaited him.

Meanwhile, in a neighboring kingdom, the obá had died without children to carry on his reign. The obá's babalawos consulted Ifá to seek a successor to the throne and were told they would find their new king naked in a forest next to a fire. With this, the babalawos quickly dispatched soldiers to the four directions in search of this man.

After wandering for days, plumes of smoke led the soldiers to the man they were seeking, where they found him just as Ifá had foretold. The soldiers clothed the young prince and brought him back to their kingdom to be crowned as the new obá.

Years later the banished prince returned home at the head of a huge army. His father went forward and knelt before the obá who then revealed himself to be his own exiled son. After a tearful reunion, the obá returned to his adopted home to reign in peace and prosperity for many years.[1]

"The patient man will be made King of the World."

Adechina had little time to waste. Through Ifá divination, the young babalawo from the crumbling empire of Oyó had been warned about the slavers who were on their way to capture him and drag him away in chains to a life of slavery. Adechina pushed away thoughts of making a run for it as he prepared to feed his Ifá tools with the blood from the two dark hens in anticipation for the daunting task that lay before him. He was resigned to his fate, as Ifá had already warned him any attempt to escape would be futile. And his own oddun in Ifá, which had appeared on the day of his initiation, foretold that he was to lose everything in order to achieve his true destiny. Adechina knew what he needed to do and he was determined to do it, no matter the cost.

Adechina tore feathers from the back of the birds' necks and let them fall onto Ifá as he chanted a traditional song we use in preparation for the sacrifice, *"Yakiña, yakiña ikú Olorun, bara yakiña."*[2] He pulled on the skin on his throat in acknowledgment that one day his life would be taken just as surely as that of the little hen he was dispatching to the other world. *"Ogún chorochoro* (Ogún's work is very difficult)."* He then proceeded to pour the warm blood of the hens over his Ifá, adding palm oil and honey over his ekines to finish nourishing the material representation of the god of wisdom and knowledge he worshiped as a priest. *"Epó malero, epó malero. Ayalá epó malero,"*[3] he sang as he added the final ingredients to the mix.

Finally, with his Ifá now properly fed, he got down to the grueling task at hand. One by one he began to take the blood-covered oil palm nuts and proceeded to swallow them, the blood and palm oil now acting as a much-needed lubricant to help choke them down. In this way he would be taking his Ifá, hidden within his own body, to accompany him on the grim journey that awaited him. His plans were already set. Once on board the slave ship he would sooner or later pass the ekin nuts, whereupon he would set about painstakingly cleaning them and hiding them on his body. Through pain and prophecy and animal sacrifice, as well as determined self-sacrifice, Ifá made the arduous journey to Cuba smuggled within Adechina's own body.

The Yorubaland of Adechina's time was quite different than it is today in a number of important ways. In Adechina's day there was no such thing as a Yoruba nation, but merely a group of people and nations in the Southwestern part of what is now Nigeria. Up until the mid-1800s there was not a Yoruba identity, only a large number of nations organized in the form of city/states that spoke various dialects of the same root language. They also claimed a shared origin in the spiritual capital of Ilé Ifé, whose progenitor, Oduduwa, had come to Ilé Ifé from somewhere in the East. Finally, they shared the belief in a large pantheon of gods and goddesses, called orichas, who rule over the forces of nature and various human endeavors. Instead of a Yoruba nation there was the Egbado, the Egba, the Ijebu, Ibadan, the Owo, the Ijesha, and Oyó, among others, who were in a constant state of flux with shifting alliances and antagonisms being the norm.

Christian missionaries first conceived the idea of a Yoruba identity in an effort to unite these disparate peoples, and the word Yoruba itself is a term borrowed from the Hausa peoples to the North, who used it to describe the people of Oyó. These same missionaries also created the first Yoruba dictionaries in their bid to mold the various city/states into a single, albeit Christian, Yoruba identity.[4] In each area they would often worship different orichas, or the same oricha might even have a completely different name. Each oricha cult competed with all the others, and priests of different orichas never formally interacted with each other or participated in each other's ceremonies. Each oricha sect also had their own religious center in the form of *igbos* (sacred groves) where major ceremonies and initiations were performed. These igbos carried the name of the oricha, so you would have an igbo Ochún, an igbo Yemayá, an igbo Obatalá, and so on. These igbos were extremely private, and only priests of the oricha were allowed to enter. Not even the priests of other orichas were permitted entrance. The only exceptions were the babalawos and the obá who were considered high priests to all the oricha groups.

The orichas who enjoyed a wide popularity had their religious centers, or capitals, as well. For example, the worship of Ochún, who in Africa is considered the oricha of the river bearing her name (in Cuba she is regarded as the owner of all fresh or sweet waters), was based in Oshogbo in what is now known as Ogun State, even though she was worshipped in igbos all over Yorubaland. And Changó, the Warrior oricha of fire, thunder, and dance hailed from the great empire of Oyó. Some orichas, like Oshossi, might be extremely popular in one area, but travel a hundred miles, and he might be completely unheard of.

The ceremonies and rituals for the worship of each of the orichas differed from one another, and the priesthoods of the various oricha groups didn't intermingle often, nor would they share their secrets with one another. The worship of even the same oricha might differ from area to area, with rituals specific to each area being incorporated. New rituals and changes to current rituals sometimes arose, not out of whim or convenience, but most often to commemorate an important event where the oricha had intervened on behalf of the people of that particular city or out of great need. One became a worshipper of an oricha in one of three ways: through family lineage where one's parents, grandparents, or other relatives were worshippers of that oricha, by becoming possessed by an oricha, or if directed to worship an oricha by Ifá.

Ifá divination, which speaks for all the orichas as well as Olodumare, was by far the most important and most trusted oracle in Yorubaland. Followers of the different orichas, including their priests, would regularly consult with babalawos on every major aspect of life. Infants were regularly brought to an Ifá priest a few days after birth to learn the innermost nature of the child and which oricha the child should grow up to worship. While the oricha cults employed their own form of divination called *merindilogún* using sixteen cowrie shells specially consecrated for this purpose, it was mainly used on ritual occasions to learn the will of the particular oricha being consulted. Although the sixteen cowrie shell divination system was derived from Ifá, it was far simpler, having only sixteen odduns of which only twelve could be read, with clients being sent to a babalawo if one of the other four odduns appeared.[5]

In fact, Ifá was the one thread that held these separate cults together as a systematic whole. Only within the body of knowledge called Ifá did the various orichas and their worship exist together in one place or achieve a cohesive whole. Histories, prayers, *orikis* (prayers in the form of praise chants), and rituals for the various orichas were all recorded in the massive compendium of oral tradition that was Ifá. This would later prove crucial when the Yorubas were forced to re-create these practices as slaves in the harsh, alien world called Cuba.

An old Chinese curse, "May you live in interesting times," is supposed to be one of the worst curses that can be inflicted on a person, and most eras that are interesting to historians are indeed horrific to those who are unfortunate enough to live in them. The 1820s Yorubaland that Adechina was living in was one of the most interesting times in the entire history of Yoruba culture. The great Oyó Empire was actively involved in the European slave trade and tearing itself apart from the inside, with the royal family engaging in intrigues that would make Machiavelli or the Roman Caesars blush, having gone through five *Alafins* (Emperors) in less than twenty years. Many of the nations who had lived peacefully under Oyó rule for so many years were now in open revolt. When not warring amongst themselves and the kingdom of Dahomey, they were making regular incursions into Oyó territory in search of slaves and conquest. From the north the Muslim Fulani were attacking, and the dark hand of European colonialism was reaching toward Oyó, grasping at the neck of Yoruba culture. Ambition and greed became so overwhelming in the Oyó Empire that the Alafin Awole, who had come into power by murdering his own father, went so far as to violate the sacred oath made by every Alafin never to attack their spiritual homeland of Ifé, by sending his top general Afonje to lay siege to the market town of Apomu in 1795. This led to a mutiny led by Afonje himself.

This order pushed the popular and powerful Afonje over the threshold, and the general and his army mutinied against the Alafin. Soon after, the Alafin Awole was sentenced to death by suicide by the babalawos of the Royal Council, known as the Oyó Mesi, for his crimes after consulting with Ifá. An unrepentant Alafin Awole cursed his own people by shooting arrows into the four directions and damning his own rebellious subjects to be carried off as slaves to the four directions, just as the arrows that he had dispatched. In short, the Yoruba world was collapsing.

The number of Yoruba slaves brought to the New World primarily came in two waves. The first took place around the 1770s, and the second and greater of the two occurred in the 1820s, which is almost certainly when Adechina was brought to Cuba. The first wave, which coincided with the opening of the slave port in Lagos, had Yorubas comprising fifty-eight percent of the slaves being brought over. The collapsing Oyo Empire was largely responsible for the second wave where Yorubas made up eighty-one percent of the slaves being sent to Havana.

Although the Spanish signed a treaty with the British to end the slave trade in 1817, illegal slave ships regularly evaded British and Spanish blockades to deliver slaves to Cuba. Though officially illegal, the slave trade to Cuba was burgeoning, and between 1826 and 1850 more than 65,000 Yoruba slaves were brought to Cuba, and it wasn't until 1867 that the last slave ship landed in Cuba.

As we saw, when the slavers came to drag Adechina off to a life of slavery, he swallowed his Ifá implements, concealing them inside his own body. Who were the slavers who captured Adechina? Were they invaders from Dahomey or another Yoruba kingdom, or was the raid perpetrated from Oyó itself? If so, was this act produced from the Alafin's unbridled greed or was it caused by yet another palace intrigue in revenge for some slight, real or imagined? Sadly, we may never know.

We don't know the exact year Adechina arrived in Cuba, as the slave ship that carried him was illegal and undocumented, but it was most likely in the late 1820s. We do know that upon his arrival in Cuba he was given the name Remigio Herrera, his surname being taken from Miguel Antonio Herrera, who owned the massive Samson y Unión plantation. We also know that with his exceptional intelligence Adechina was eventually able to win the favor of his masters and insinuate himself into their good graces. This was rewarded by him being allowed enough freedom to serve as a courier, running errands between his owners' plantation near Matanzas and the capital of La Habana. It was on one of his trips that he stumbled upon another enslaved babalawo, Adé Bí, who had arrived some time after Adechina.

Adé Bí, whose own oddun was Ojuani Boka, had also gained favor with his masters, but in his case, it was directly through his abilities as an Ifá diviner. He had gained the trust of his own masters through the use of an ecuele he had constructed out of dried orange peels and a string taken from a majagua bush, which he used to advise his masters on their various business negotiations. Because of the accuracy of his predictions, Adé Bí gained the full trust of his masters and was permitted to come and go almost at the will. Eventually, he was given his freedom because of his help in predicting the outcome of a particularly large deal for his owners through Ifá divination.

During their conversation, Adechina informed Adé Bí that he had managed to smuggle his Ifá into Cuba and that it needed to be ritually washed and fed. Due to the esteem that Adé Bí's owners held him in, it was not difficult for the babalawo to procure the basement of a bodega in which to do the cleaning and feeding. Two days later, Adechina divined with the newly washed and fed ekin nuts as is traditionally done, and the oddun that came up was his own sign, Obara Meyi.[6] Probably sometime in the late 1820s, other Lucumí slaves recognizing Adechina's stature as an Ifá priest got together and bought his freedom. Soon afterward he founded a *cabildo* (religious council) in the Simpson district of Matanzas, where he worked as a babalawo and began his meteoric rise among the Lucumí religious community in Cuba.

The babalawos' training had imparted in them an encyclopedic knowledge of the various orichas, their rites, prayers, and the relationships between them. This became the crucial link necessary in recreating the complex religious world among the Lucumí slaves whose cultural and spiritual identity had been shattered by the institutionalized terrorism of slavery. Central to achieving these ends was the institution known as the *cabildo de nación* (ethnic councils).

The Spanish encouraged them to form these cabildos and saw them as a means of control and to prevent the possibility of slave uprisings. For the Lucumís the cabildos became central to the survival and re-creation of their culture and religion on the island. They served as mutual aid organizations, amassing funds to buy their brethren out of slavery and to aid the sick, the infirm, the elderly, and those in need. Just as they had done in Africa and in many indigenous cultures throughout the world, the babalawos and the santeros did much of their rituals and work on behalf of the community in which they served. This is underscored on the Ifá side by the vow to serve humanity made by every babalawo during their initiation. For example, leading up to the New Year, the babalawos gather to perform a number of ceremonies and feed the different positions of the world for the Opening of the Year ceremony. This is done to ensure the well-being of the community and the whole world.

We conduct special rituals for Orun, the sea, the river, the sun, the moon, the stars, the wind, the hills, the rainbow, the dawn, the cemetery, waterspouts, certain sacred trees, and so on, and they are all fed in the process. These huge ebbós are called Olubo Borotiri Baba Ebbó, or Father of All Sacrifices, as they are for the entire world. This all culminates in the babalawos performing deep divination to find out the Ifá oddun that rules the year, which is now published by many of the world's newspapers. After weeks of ceremonies, a tambor begins for the orichas, and everyone is welcome to this party. The cabildos became a little piece of Africa with the focus always on the well-being of the community and the world. These cabildos exerted a tremendous amount of influence on how the religion is practiced, even to this day. Nearly all of the Lucumí cabildos were founded and run by a commanding combination of babalawos and powerful santeras who conducted the vast majority of ceremonies up until the 1930s, many of whom were also married to babalawos. Later, as the age of the cabildos faded to a close great babalawos such as Tata Gaitán, who would later become installed as the obá over the religion, operated their own homes under the same principle of aid to the community that had guided the great cabildos.

The reconstruction of oricha worship in Cuba entailed great changes from the independent, competitive oricha cults of Africa. In Africa most priests did not receive orichas to take to their homes upon their initiation. Instead the orichas remained at the main igbo center of their particular oricha. This form is now all but non-existent in Cuba. Those who did directly receive orichas received only their oricha and Elegguá, a practice called *cabeza y pie* (head and foot) in Cuba. This head and foot initiation eventually gave way to the *kariocha* (initiation ceremony), introduced by the powerful Havana santera Efunché, where Eleggua (Elegba), Obatalá, Ochún, Yemayá, and Changó were received along with the initiate's Olorí (tutelary oricha).[7] In Cuba's new compressed initiation process, the initiations to the various orichas, which were often very different from one another in Nigeria, were now all performed using the initiation to Changó as a model with minor variations to accommodate the various orichas. The babalawos participated heavily in these ceremonies, at times being charged with performing everything from the pre-initiation consultation and *Ebbó de Entrada* (Entering Sacrifice) to cleanse the initiate-to-be before entering the initiation room, to shaving the neophyte's head, blessing the plants used in the ceremony, and performing the animal sacrifice.[8] The very name of the room where oricha initiations are held, igbodún, is a testament to the enormous influence of these babalawos. Igbodún is what they called the Ifá grove in Africa.

Of course, with great change comes great struggles between different factions, and babalawos played their part in those as well. Miguel Ramos's fascinating paper *La Division de la Habana*, depicts in great detail one such epic war between the great priestess Ma Monserrate (Obatero) who battled for supremacy against the combined forces of two other exceptionally powerful priestesses, Latuán and Efunché. When Ma Monserrate lost the war, it was Adechina who accompanied her to Matanzas and installed her at the helm of the cabildo he had founded soon after gaining his freedom. He topped it off by commissioning a set of batá drums from the babalawo and co-founder of the drumming tradition Atanda, playing them in a tambor to commemorate her inauguration as the new head of the cabildo.

The babalawos were instrumental in reviving the sacred music of Africa as well. The batá drumming tradition was created in Cuba when the babalawo Atanda partnered with another drummer, Aña Bí, to consecrate the first batá drums in Cuba, and teach others in the religion the complex rhythms needed to praise and bring down the orichas to possess their initiates. In Matanzas the oral tradition insists the drumming tradition there was transmitted by none other than Adechina himself.

Of course, Ifá itself had to be reconstructed on the island, but here the babalawos had an almost insurmountable hurdle to overcome. The babalawos now realized they had an immense problem on their hands. If they didn't initiate new babalawos, the secrets of Ifá in Cuba would go to the grave with them. The physical secrets of Odun (commonly referred to as Olófin), a manifestation of the Supreme Being and the highest power in Ifá are, like the orichas, received physically by the initiate and are absolutely necessary for the initiation, but they didn't exist in Cuba. Therefore, it was impossible to initiate a new babalawo without her being present in the igbodún (igbo Odun or Odun's grove), the initiation room named after her. Not only would any attempt to initiate a new babalawo without her presence be a grave disrespect and sacrilege to her, the ceremony would not be recognized by Ifá and would therefore be worthless. So the only way new babalawos could be initiated in Cuba was for a babalawo to risk everything to return to Africa to receive Odun, and then attempt to sneak back into Cuba with her. Even the best possible scenario would involve months of enduring the difficulties of sea in each direction. And there was the very real possibility of jail or death if anything went wrong. Although the attempt to return to Africa and smuggle Odun back into Cuba was incredibly dangerous, plans began to be hatched and refined in secret. Most babalawos agree it was Adechina himself who made the attempt using the code name Odun, and in fact received Odun/Olófin twice while he was in Africa.

The first babalawos to come to Cuba knew Odun was absolutely essential to the initiation of new Ifá priests. If you add to this the extreme hardships these babalawos were willing to endure in order to bring Odun to Cuba, it becomes much easier to understand why Cuban babalawos are adamant in refusing to recognize any Ifá Priest initiated without her being in the room. That point is simply non-negotiable for us, and it is difficult for us to view it as anything but an outrageous insult, not only to our traditions, but also to the early babalawos such as Adechina who went to such lengths to preserve them. To us, the lives of the slaves who acted with such courage and brilliance have worth, and we are offended by those who imply that they don't.

Once Odun was smuggled into Cuba it was possible for new babalawos to be initiated, and Adechina initiated several Africans such as Ño Akonkón Oluguery (Oyekun Meyi) and Ño Blas Cárdenas (also Oyekun Meyi), as well as one or two Cuban-born Creoles.[9] In turn, Oluguery initiated the famous Eulogio Rodriguez "Tata" Gaitán, who is considered the head of the particular *rama* (Ifá line or branch) I belong to, with Adechina acting as the oyugbona, or second padrino. Unfortunately, Oluguery was not able to fully train Tata Gaitán as he left Cuba to return to Africa, dying in Mexico during the attempt, which left Tata Gaitán to get much of his training from Oluguery's brother in Ifá, Ño Blas Cárdenas.

During this same period in the 1860s, Adechina moved to Regla, which is across the bay from Havana. There he founded the famous cabildo de la Virgen de Regla, the saint associated with the oricha of the sea Yemayá, thus helping to give root to Ifá in the Havana area with it eventually becoming the stronghold of Ifá in Cuba. Over the years, Adechina became such a revered and powerful babalawo that people from all walks of life were known to spontaneously kneel and kiss his hand when they would encounter him on the street. Up until his death on January 27, 1905, Adechina selflessly taught his godchildren and their godchildren. After his death, Adechina's cabildo was led by his daughter Josefina, affectionately known as Pepa, and became famous for the massive processions they would hold for Yemayá every September 7 (the feast day for the Virgin de Regla) with batá drums layered with the songs sung in her honor.

I chose to put the pataki taken from Adechina's oddun at the beginning of this chapter to illustrate how closely Adechina's life followed his oddun in Ifá, Obara Meyi. Every babalawo is born as a child or personification of one of the Ifá odduns. As expected, the child of Obara Meyi is almost certainly predestined to lose everything up to, and even including, their very clothes, only to rise again over time like a phoenix from its ashes to become even greater than before. Adechina lost everything when he became enslaved and drug off to Cuba, but over time he was able to achieve a greatness and success in Cuba that he may not have achieved if he had remained in Africa. Obara Meyi is also an oddun of wisdom where the chain of learning from teacher to pupil was born just as most of Cuban Ifá comes from Adechina's teachings. This oddun is also one of the principle signs of commerce and financial success that certainly came to the ex-slave Adechina, giving us an outstanding example of how the events and traits in a person's life will reflect the oddun they embody.

Adechina was truly a great babalawo not merely due to his seemingly inexhaustible wealth of knowledge, wisdom and compassion, but because Ifá and babalawos would not even exist in Cuba if it weren't for his selfless actions. His willingness to risk life and limb—not once but twice—to give birth to Ifá in Cuba and nurture it to fruition is just now bearing fruit. Thanks to him, Santería is now a world religion and a treasured part of Cuban heritage and culture.

In an ironic twist, Santería has now come to the aid of the religion in Africa itself, as the explosion of interest in Santería has led more and more people to explore the religion's roots. In turn, the sudden leap in interest from outsiders has caused many Yorubas, taught to look upon their own religious roots as backwards and primitive, to look at their heritage with new eyes and with a renewed sense of pride. Oricha worship in Yorubaland, which was in serious decline due to the effects of colonialism and the attitudes that came with it, is now growing by leaps and bounds.

Adechina (Obara Meyi)

Chapter Five
Lucumí

There was a time when all the orichas lived apart from one another, each one living in their own land, ruling as kings and queens. In those days, nobody knew of any orichas outside of their own territory.

This was an era when Death roamed the earth, dressed all in black and performing her grim work in the cover of night. In the confusion of darkness, Death could take anyone she wanted, and only Oggun and Oshun's territories seemed to be exempt from her predations. This attracted the attention of the other orichas, so they held a meeting where they decided to go to the house of a famous Man of Knowledge who lived in Ara Ifé Ocha, to try to get to the bottom of this situation.

When they arrived, they saw that this Man of Knowledge was divining using dark seeds split in two and connected with a chain. He also wore a necklace of green and yellow beads. They didn't know why he used these things, but they looked suspiciously like those used by Ochún and Oggún, and the chain looked just like the one Death used to tie up her victims. None of the orichas dared to report their suspicions to Olófin out of fear that this Wise One might be a friend of Death's.

This went on for some time, until one day Obatalá appeared on earth, saying, "I trust I am not late."

After the orichas finished saluting Obatalá, he continued, "I am Olófin's representative, and in accordance with Olófin, I envelop the good and I expose the evil. You have not dared to say anything about this Wise Man because you feared he might be a friend of Death; therefore, I was forced to come here."

Obatalá looked up toward the heavens, saying, "I was given sixteen rays of sunlight by Olófin and was ordered to seek unification among all of you. But due to your lack of understanding and each of you believing you have more power than the other, the results have not been good even after such a long time.

"Here we are, in the sacred house of Ifá where Olófin also lives. This place you do not wish to acknowledge, because you don't wish to recognize that this Wise Man you see before you is the direct spokesperson of Olófin, here to deliver Olófin's mandates and to whom Olófin has entrusted her powers. This old Wise One, whose name is ... Orunmila."

At this, Orunmila came over and saluted Obatalá and proceeded to consult Ifá. The oddun that appeared demanded they immediately bring the green and yellow beads together and put a white flag up in the house. He went on to explain that the green was his own identifying color and that the yellow belonged to Ochún, who represents half the world, gold, the blood that runs through our veins, and life itself. The seeds and the chain belonged to Oggún, who represents the other half of the world and who is the oricha of death by order of Olófin.

He continued, "That is why Death has not killed anyone here in Ara Ifé Ocha. Now that you acknowledge Olófin's wishes that you unite and recognize me today, tomorrow, and for always, I will put these idefás (Ifá bracelets) on each of you so you will be under my protection and so the doors will always be open for the children of Olófin."

Ever since then, the orichas have lived together, and to this day this unification is reflected in the homes of santeros and babalawos, where you can see the orichas living together in the same canastillero cabinets.

"The lives of all who have passed away are in the memory of Ifá."

When Adechina and so many other oricha priests were brought to Cuba as slaves, they were determined to re-create their culture in this hostile new land, but they faced monumental hurdles along the way. In Africa, every oricha had their own religion with their own initiation ceremony, each very different than the other orichas, and only priests of that particular oricha and babalawos were allowed to attend the ceremonies.

Therefore, in Yorubaland you had, and still have, hundreds, maybe even thousands of orichas, each with their own separate religions. But the chances were slim to none that Yoruba culture would survive in Cuba in this form. So their culture might persevere, the *alagua laguas* (highly respected elders) formed mutual aid societies organized as cabildos, and created a new Lucumí culture where a number of major adaptations were conceived.

Using the knowledge found in Ifá's odduns, combined with the ritual knowledge remembered by the most respected oricha priestesses and priests, they organized the orichas into a pantheon based on the relationships found in Ifá's patakís. This was a major development because now instead of having many oricha religions as in Africa, the Lucumís had constructed one religion for the many orichas. This process, however, was often anything but smooth as various factions wielded their considerable power in defense of the traditions they held dear. In fact, not long after Ña Monserrate (Obatero) was forced to relocate to Matanzas with the help of Adechina, she found herself embroiled in another epic battle of wills ... and orichas.

Living in Matanzas was a powerful santero by the name of Ño José Ikúdaisí. With Ño José, the personal relationships santeros and babalawos have with the orichas took a very strange twist. For some unknown reason, Yemayá had somehow angered Ño José Ikúdaisí, and he had vowed never to have anything to do with the powerful oricha of the seas! When the parents of the now-famous Ferminita Gomez took their daughter to be initiated, Ño José Ikúdaisí refused to initiate her to Yemayá, consecrating her to Ochún with the name Ocha Bí instead. Soon after her initiation, things began to go horribly for her. A short time later, Ferminita Ocha Bí went to Obatero's cabildo to seek help. The elder santera saw the young initiate with the shells, and during the consultation it came up that the source of Ferminita's troubles was that she had been initiated to the wrong oricha and that she should have been consecrated to Yemayá. Ña Monserrate immediately took the steps necessary to re-initiate Ocha Bí to Yemayá. Of course this did not sit well with Ikúdaisí, and it was only a matter of days before the war began. In Matanzas people still talk about this war that was fought not only on a political realm, but in the realm of the orichas between two extremely powerful santeros.

The opening battle began when one night Ikúdaisí went to the door of the Obatero's to perform a magical ritual to teach Obatero a lesson, but his plans were dashed when Changó possessed the sleeping Obatero who ran to the door to confront Ikúdaisí. Finding himself face-to-face with the enraged Changó, the santero was scared out of his wits. Accounts say that he stumbled, fell, and then ran all the way home in a panic. Changó then performed rituals to remove the *ogu* (witchcraft). When Changó left Ña Monserrate's body, she was confused and had to be informed what had transpired by her neighbors who had been awakened by the uproar. When the santera was told what had happened, she was furious.[1]

This war went on for months until finally one day Changó showed he had less patience than his daughter Obatero. He again possessed the santera and grabbing an *eduara* (thunder stone), Changó openly stomped over to Ikúdaisí's house in the middle of the day. Standing right in Ikúdaisí's doorway, the mighty oricha held up the thunder stone and began to roar prayers to the heavens. Immediately, the skies began to darken and a huge thunderstorm erupted over Matanzas, and Changó stomped off. Moments afterward a lightning bolt hit right on the spot where the oricha had been standing. The next day Ikúdaisí died mysteriously and Obatero was considered the winner of the war.[2]

Through agreements, alliances, struggles, and outright wars such as this one the Lucumí religion was formed. It was now organized in such a way that the familial relationships between the orichas were emphasized. For instance, in Nigeria Yemayá is the oricha of the Ogún River whose worship is centered at Abeokuta, while Ochún rules the Ochún River, having her center of worship at Oshogbo. In Lucumí, we emphasize the relationships where, for example, Yemayá and Ochún are sisters with Yemayá ruling over the seas and Ochún presiding over all the fresh water such as streams and rivers. Many of the details of the orichas' relationships with one another are recounted in the *itáns* (histories or parables) found in Ifá.

The alagua lagua elders also condensed the many initiation ceremonies into a core ceremony, which they based largely on initiation rituals for Changó that had been brought from Oyó. From this core they made adaptations to accommodate specific rituals and ingredients for each of the orichas. Finally, they expanded the kariocha so the initiate would receive a number of orichas instead of just one. This was an important adaptation because there is a general rule in the religion that you can't view or work with an oricha that you have not actually received yourself. So with each santera or santero receiving a number of orichas during their initiation, it became possible for them to participate in initiations for all the different orichas. This innovation gave the Lucumí religion the flexibility needed to ensure the survival of the different orichas in Cuba. In Lucumí, priests of all the different orichas come together to form a community who interact and participate in ceremonies for each of the orichas. During the Lucumí kariocha the new initiate receives several orichas and all the orichas are saluted, prayed, and sung to during the ceremony. This is very different from Nigeria where only priests of one oricha are allowed to be present. The only exception is that babalawos may participate in the various ceremonies for the different orichas due to their exclusive knowledge of all the deities. To this day it is still next to impossible to perform initiations in the New World in the way they are done in Yorubaland.

Traditionally in Yorubaland, oricha priests often did not receive their orichas in full to take home with them. Instead they worshipped their oricha at the igbo where they were initiated and often only received a consecrated tool to take home with them. For example, the Obatalá priest Salakọ in William Bascom's *Sixteen Cowries* described how new priests were given only a piece of bone or ivory to take home with them, and though many priests could be mounted (possessed) only the official ẹlẹgún could actually speak. For many of the cults in Yorubaland, the idea of receiving the oricha as part of the initiation process was undesirable and even nonsensical. Why give birth to and worship a young version of the oricha when you could go to the shrine and directly worship the ancient one that has been worshipped and gained power there for centuries? Many of the oricha religions would also look upon the idea of receiving one's own oricha in full as being overly individualistic, which in turn could threaten the position of the main shrine and its internal hierarchy of priestesses and priests. In Cuba on the other hand, a single centralized shrine would constantly be in danger of being confiscated or destroyed by the white ruling class. With every priest having their own oricha, each santera became their own secret cell of the religion.

It must be remembered that besides being a religion and a culture, Santería was also very much a resistance movement where slaves could actively oppose the slave owners' culture by secretly retaining and living their own culture. In fact, the plots to initiate several armed uprisings were born in the Lucumí cabildos, such as the famous Cabildo Changó Tedún, whose leader José Antonio Aponte is said to have attempted a massive rebellion in 1812. Merely being in the religion was considered an act of resistance in and of itself by both blacks and whites. And during many periods in Cuban history, santeras and santeros had to keep the religion very much underground to avoid the harsh punishment, or even death, they might receive if they were discovered.

Also very importantly, the Yoruba drumming traditions were brought to the shores of Cuba and spread by babalawos such as the master carver, drummer, and Ifá priest Atanda (Baba Eyiogbe), the master drummer Añá Bí, and Adechina himself.[3, 4] The consecration of the drums as well as the rhythms of the orichas became particularly strong for the batá drumming tradition, with its three drums consecrated to the oricha Añá by babalawos. In Africa the rhythms played on the batá drums were for Changó and eggun, so the other orichas' rhythms had to be adapted to the batá drums. Other drums, although rarely seen these days, such as those for Olokun, were also built, consecrated, and played by babalawos who passed on their knowledge to Cuban santeros.

Less significant changes were also made, such as in some of the *ewe and eran* (plants and animals) to accommodate the fact that not all of the plants and animals used in Africa could be found in Cuba. The most crucial plants, such as the plants known as achés, which are indispensable for initiations, were imported from Africa and others were either substituted or dropped altogether. The Native American influence on Santería is most strikingly noticeable in the use of two of their most sacred plants, corn and tobacco, in many rituals. Corn, although of Native American origin, is now used ritually by the Yorubas in Nigeria as well.

The hybrid makeup of the Anagó or Lucumí language mirrors the coming together of the various Yoruba, Native American, and Spanish cultures that came to define the Lucumí culture, allowing our cultures to survive and even thrive in extremely hostile territory. The Anagó/ Lucumí language is derived from a number of Yoruba cultures such as Oyó, Ifé, Iyesa (Ijesha), Takua, Iyebú (Ijebú), and Egguado (Egbado) with influences from other Afro-Cuban cultures such as Arará (Fon), Bantu, Taino Indian, and the Cuban Creole culture with Spanish influence. The language was altered to accommodate the different Yoruba dialects, particularly the Oyó and Egbado influence. Most noticeable was the new Lucumí/Anagó dialect's loss of the Yoruba languages' tonal structure, which was replaced with accents taken from the main Cuban language, which is Spanish. Although many times the accents would approximate those tones to some degree, the Spanish influence remains strong.

Since much of the Anagó/Lucumí language is based on a mixture of dialects from at least 200 years ago when the Yorubas were brought to Cuba en masse, we must sound very strange to modern day Yorubas. Despite the dated and mixed dialect, some Lucumís were still able to hold conversations with Yoruba sailors they encountered landing at Cárdenas port in Matanzas, Cuba as recently as the 1950s. But since the Lucumí dialect is based on a version of Yoruba that is more than 200 years old, the Lucumí speakers must have sounded much like a person from the days of the American Revolution would sound to us today in the United States.

The different dialects, as well as oró iyinle, archaic words used in secret aspects of odduns such as incantations, were brought together to help form a new Yoruba-Cuban language called Anagó. In similar ways, the alagua laguas who headed the cabildos pulled together the various regional Yoruba oricha cults to forge a religion with a condensed pantheon of the most important orichas from the various regions of Yorubaland. Modern English became much more than the Anglo and Saxon Germanic languages after it absorbed Norse and local British languages as well as the French of the Norman invaders. In a similar way, Lucumí culture became more than its source culture by forging the elements of all the cultures affecting them to create a unique Lucumí cultural identity.

Several aspects of the Lucumí culture and religion never existed in Cuba or Africa before being created by the alagua laguas in Cuba in the 1800s and early 1900s as well.

In his truly ground breaking work *The Cooking of History*, Palmié revealed how ethnologists, starting with Fernando Ortiz in the 1930s and carried on by virtually every ethnologist since, made Santería valid by showing how its roots came from the Yoruba peoples of what is now southwest Nigeria. Marveling at how much of the language and culture had been retained by babalawos and santeros, the researchers began to look everywhere for signs of Yoruba culture, which was immediately noticed by the santeros themselves. Those studying the santeros refused to see the santeros' agency in assuming the aspects of Western culture that suited their own needs and desires, or more importantly, that the way the santeros used Western culture for their own ends was an act of resistance in and of itself. The early babalawos' and santeros' genius in their artful repurposing of Western and Christian culture allowed the orichas to not only survive but to thrive in the Diaspora, whereas in the African homeland oricha worship is barely surviving. Ethnologists since Ortiz have thus focused almost exclusively on the Yoruba aspects of the religion that had an unintended effect on the very religion they were studying. Santeros, now seeing that the Yoruba aspects of their religion gave them a new found validity, began to alter the religion to make it more Yoruba so they might gain more acceptability and respect from Cuban society. Certain babalawos and santeros went as far as to take information they found in the ethnologists' own libraries and adding it to the religion to make it more Yoruba.[5] The ethnologists were thus responsible for the Yorubization of the religion, and over the years more and more santeros accepted the ethnologists' myth that Santería was a somehow degraded form of a pure Yoruba religion, and have continued to try to change the religion to fit this warped viewpoint. Unfortunately, this myth is still believed by many ethnologists and santeros alike.

Although changes were certainly made to ensure the survival of the religion, remarkably the Lucumí alagua laguas managed to preserve rituals and rules of the religion that now appear to have been lost even in their homeland in Africa. Wande Abimbola, who is the *Awishe* (official spokesperson) for all of African Ifá, acknowledges in his book *Ifá Will Mend a Broken World* that the Diaspora managed to keep alive a number of the rituals and rules that have been forgotten in Africa.

William Bascom is widely considered to have been the foremost academic authority on the Yoruba up until his death in 1981.[6] Bascom, along with his Cuban-born ethnologist wife, spent years studying the religion in Havana and Matanzas. Bascom and his famous French colleague Pierre Fatumbi Verger are known for writing the most intensive studies comparing Yoruba and New World versions of Ifá and oricha worship to date. In 1965 Bascom came to the startling conclusion that the religion is actually much stronger in Cuba than it is in Yorubaland. Further, Bascom agreed with Verger on his prediction that before long the Yoruba might be traveling to Cuba or Brazil to learn about their own religion.

That prediction came true fifteen years later in the form of none other than the Ooni of Ifé, traditional spiritual and political ruler over the entire Yoruba people, and the Awishe Abimbola. Scholar and obá oriaté Miguel Ramos affirms he was present at a 1980 meeting where Wande Abimbola informed the group that he had been sent there on a mission by the Ooni. He was to investigate the oricha Traditions in the Western Hemisphere to see how New World priests could aid in recuperating some of what had been lost in Africa.[7] Remembering such details is strong evidence that the differences we see in traditional Lucumí were well-thought-out changes, rather than the kind of haphazard ones that would result in the kind of degradation and loss of ritual knowledge that would befit the accusations that are sometimes leveled against the Lucumís. It also points to the oft-neglected fact that Yoruba culture changed in Africa as well as it had in the New World.

Cultures, like languages, are living things that grow and change. As they come in contact with each other, they adapt and borrow from one another. The Yorubas absorbed elements of culture from other Yoruba subgroups, neighboring nations, as well as influence from colonialists.

The Lucumís in turn melded a number of Yoruba cultures and languages, along with aspects of other African cultures that had come to Cuba, as well as some Taino Indian and Spanish influence. Therefore, effectively the Lucumí religion might be considered in some ways to be a regional variation, but still its own entity.

The effects of colonialism and slavery were every bit as damaging for the Yorubas who remained in Africa as it was for the slaves taken to Cuba. For instance, slave raids became so extreme that entire towns were burned to the ground with every member of the town being sold into slavery. It has been said that virtually the entire population of Ketu, the center of Ochossi worship (the oricha of the hunt), was sent into slavery in Cuba and Brazil. Thus, Ochossi almost ceased to exist in Africa because virtually all of the priests ended up in Cuba and Brazil where Ochossi became an important oricha. The ability to accommodate and adapt useful aspects of other cultures is one of the Yorubas' most impressive characteristics.

It is probably this trait that helped the early slaves to adapt to their new world so successfully when they created the Lucumí religion. And, most famously, the early Lucumís cleverly hid their religion behind the guise of the Catholic saints that they had been forced to worship, causing the religion to be known as Santería and its priests as santeras/os. But the early Lucumís went much farther than to merely hide the orishas behind the saints. They deliberately subverted Christianity to fit their own culture. Using only the aspects of the western religion they found useful and which fit their own worldview, the Lucumís changed Christianity to fit into a Lucumí framework rather than the other way around. To find evidence of this, you simply have to ask a santera or santero to describe any of the saints. You will quickly realize they are not describing a saint at all, but an oricha. And you will be hard pressed to find a santera who is able to describe even the most basic characteristics or history of any Catholic saints. Furthermore, you will find virtually no evidence of Christian concepts or worldview in Santería. So rather than the saints and name Santería being evidence of Lucumí submission to a conquest by slave owners, instead we find an intentional subversion of the western religion which became an act of resistance in and of itself.

These adaptations gave the Lucumí religion the flexibility to survive and even thrive in its new home in Cuba. In fact, not only has this flexibility allowed Santería to survive, but to grow exponentially to become a world religion in its own right.[8]

Ifá in the United States

The first step in the globalization of the Lucumí religion was when it crossed the Florida Straits into the US. Ifá and the Lucumí religion in general came to the United States in the form of the babalawo Pancho Moro (Ifá Morote). The famous musician, Mario Bauza, would travel to Cuba regularly to receive spiritual guidance from the elder babalawo Quintín Lecón, and each time he would attempt to persuade Lecón to come to New York. Finally, in 1946, the Associación de San Francisco headed by Lecón, sent his godchild Pancho Moro to New York to bring the religion to the United States. What eventually would become a thriving Lucumí community grew up around Pancho Mora in New York. On December 4, 1955 Pancho Mora held a tambor for Changó. Two attendees, Julito Collazo and Francisco Aguabella, were religious batá drummers who had moved to New York from Cuba after a tour with the Katherine Dunham Dance Troupe. Attendees were stunned when these two began to sing the old Lucumí chants, and soon many of the attendees were packed tightly around the two, listening attentively.

Julito Collazo and Francisco Aguabella were the first sacred batá drummers to come to the United States. Julito's mother, Ebelia Collazo, was a well-known santera in Cuba who had been initiated in Regla, Cuba, by the famous and immensely powerful Latuán, who ruled over much of Havana's religious practice. Julito was extremely knowledgeable about the religion, although he was not initiated as a babalawo until the 1980s when he made his Ifá in Cuba at the hands of the famous elder Quintín Lecon, padrino of Pancho Mora. Just a couple of years later, he participated in the first *plante* (kofá and abo faca initiation ceremony) in San Francisco on August 8, 1988. It was during this ceremony that I had the good fortune of meeting Julito, who became my oyugbona.

Slowly the community began to spread from this small core of knowledgeable practitioners, but it wasn't until 1961 that the first person was initiated as a santero on US soil. The first initiation was performed in New York City by the pioneer Mercedes Nobles (Oban Yoko), a priestess of Changó, the oricha of fire, thunder, dance, and drum. During the 1960s and '70s the religion gained popularity among the growing Cuban-American population as many Cubans came to the United States to escape the revolution. Involvement in the tradition became seen by many as a measure of one's Cuban-ness and as a means to retain their Cuban identity in the alien culture of the United States. It also gave Cubans an alternative way to gain prestige; in Miami, white Cubans—who just a few years before had disparaged Santería because to them it was associated with lower-class blacks—began to be initiated as santeros and babalawos.

Although Pancho Mora arrived in 1946, the first documented priest as well as the first babalawo to come to the United States, it wasn't until 1970 that babalawos started to be initiated on US soil. Up until then, those wishing to be initiated as Ifá priests were forced to travel to Cuba to have the ceremonies performed. History repeated itself as once again, due to the absence of Odun/Olófin, initiations of new babalawos had to wait until someone could sneak the sacred attributes of Odun/Olófin into the country, this time from Cuba. Finally, a babalawo by the name of Carlos Ojeda (Osá Rete) was able to have his Olófin smuggled in from Cuba, reportedly by a Trinidadian diplomat. The first babalawos were initiated in Miami by Diego Fontela, using Ojeda's Olófin within a year. Since his was the only Olófin in the country, any babalawo who wanted to initiate someone to Ifá in the United States had to borrow Ojeda's Olófin. For years, this gave Carlos Ojeda unprecedented power in the United States as he effectively controlled who would and would not be initiated in the entire country.[9]

In the early days, there were few well-trained and experienced babalawos, olorichas, and drummers in the United States, and many of them would only teach those willing to undertake intensive apprenticeships similar to those undergone in Cuba. This kind of apprenticeship was unfamiliar to many Americans and proved to be unpopular. This led many practitioners to begin to look toward other resources to learn from, and many budding young priestesses and priests began to pore over ethnographic works such as those by Ortiz and Cabrera. These, as well as the few books written by actual practitioners, became virtual bibles for many practitioners in the United States who used them to fill the gaps in their knowledge of the religion.

Santería began to become popular outside the Cuban-American community as more and more people found themselves attracted to this alluring Cuban religion that was so deep, mysterious, and powerful. For some, particularly African-Americans, information from ethnological books about Yoruba Ifá and oricha worship began to have a greater influence, and some practitioners began to incorporate practices hailing from Africa. Others cherry-picked aspects of African practices to justify changes. For instance, some Lucumí iworos used William Bascom's *Sixteen Cowries* as evidence that they could now read all sixteen signs of the diloggún, though the same book cautioned that the vast majority of priests in Africa read only the first twelve signs just like the Lucumís.[10]

In the 1970s, as books on Ifá for the exclusive use of babalawos made their way to the open market we started seeing some santeros using the books to read the shells as if they were Ifá. Needless to say, this is hardly traditional and an insult, not only to babalawos but to the santeros who worked so hard and sacrificed so much to preserve the rich oral traditions associated with the diloggún.[11]

Some felt that if a practice was used anywhere in Yorubaland it justified grafting that practice on to their own invented forms of the religion, respecting neither the Lucumí or the African traditions. More traditional practitioners consider this to be a slap in the face of our ancestors; the slaves who displayed such courage and genius in the face of immense hardships to preserve our traditions. In fact, some consider such inventions to be the greatest single threat that our tradition faces today.

The religion began to be extremely fractured in the US, and myriad variations and inventions in religious practices began to appear, often justified with, "That's how it's done in our *ilé* (oricha house)." Many such innovations are referred to as *inventos* (inventions) or worse by many traditional Lucumí practitioners. It became more common for a godchild to leave an ilé than in Cuba, where the level of attachment, loyalty, and respect expected of a godchild is much greater. In the US it is not terribly uncommon for a godchild to remain in an ilé for only a short time and jump from ilé to ilé with great frequency. Oftentimes a person will leave an ilé when they learn the level of commitment and respect expected of them. In a traditional Cuban-style ilé, a person who is unwilling to work hard to help their godparents will simply not be taught. Other times, the fault lies with a godparent who is abusive or only interested in making money off of the godchild. Then there are what we in the religion call spiritual tourists. We have found this to be an American phenomenon where people go from religion to religion collecting initiations.

The general health of the religion improved dramatically when the Mariel Boatlift began in 1980. With the massive influx of Cubans from a wide range of races and classes came a large number of knowledgeable olorichas and babalawos. Many of them found themselves appalled at the lack of knowledge and the way rituals were being carried out in the US. If these newcomers met resistance from those who saw them as a threat to their dominions, they also found many people who were eager to learn from experienced priestesses and priests.[12] Not long after this it became somewhat easier for people to travel to Cuba, either legally with permission from the US State Department or by evading the laws and entering Cuba via Mexico or Canada. The Cuban government encouraged the surreptitious travel by not stamping the passports of Americans entering from Mexico or Canada, relying only on the Cuban visas for documentation of their entry and exit. This allowed more people to become initiated or simply go to learn in Cuba, and after 1979 exiled Cubans were allowed to enter Cuba again, and were free to connect or re-connect with elders on the island.

African-Americans were among the first to travel to Nigeria in search of an even more African form of the religion. Although many of the early pioneers had been initiated in the Lucumí tradition, the African-Americans were opposed to any traces of Christianity such as saints, which they associated with slavery. As the tradition had its roots in Yorubaland, they were eager to go to what they considered to be the source of everything in Santería, and while the oricha traditions had changed in Africa these trailblazers helped to open up a dialogue between Africa and the Diaspora. This new interest from overseas helped the struggling oricha traditions in Africa to gain popularity once more, and have been aided by their Lucumí sisters and brothers along the way.

One of the earliest pioneers, Walter Eugene King (Ofuntola), became the first African-American to become initiated as an oloricha in Matanzas, Cuba, on August 16, 1959. By October 1970, he had founded the Yoruba Village of Oyotunji in Sheldon, South Carolina. He began the careful re-organization of the Orisa vodu priesthood along the traditional Nigerian lines, becoming initiated to Ifá in Abeokuta, Nigeria, in 1972. In 1977, apparently following William Bascom's advice that the Yorubas might go to Cuba to learn about their religion, Ofuntola brought in the Lucumí oriaté Ernesto Pichardo to consecrate the orichas Babalú Ayé and Oba for Oyotunji in the Cuban tradition. In June 1981, Ofuntola returned to Nigeria, this time to the sacred city of Ifé, where he was granted an audience with the *Ooni* (King of Ifé), who ordered his coronation as an obá, and he became His Royal Majesty Obá Ofuntola Oseijeman Adelabu Adefunmi I. In the summer of 1985, he commissioned Ernesto Pichardo to initiate one of his wives as a priestess of Babalú Ayé. As Oyotunji was in need of songs for the orichas, Oyotunji's Master Drummer took advantage of Pichardo's visit to record the Lucumí songs sung by Pichardo during his visit. Thus, Oyotunji artfully combined several religious practices from the Yoruba of Nigeria, the Fon of Dahomey, and the Lucumí of Cuba to fit their needs, creating what might best be described as a kind of hybrid Orisa-Lucumí-Vodun religion.

On occasion, the differences between Santería and how the religion is now being practiced in Africa and by neo-traditionalists in the US have created friction between the groups. Sometimes these differences in rules and rituals cause many heated exchanges between the two groups. For example, in the last twenty years some areas such as Ilé Ifé have begun to initiate women as Ifá priests, which has become the cause for friction between the two groups. The neo-traditionalists claim the Lucumís are sexist for refusing to recognize women Ifá priests, and the Lucumís counter that any Ifá initiation is invalid if Odun/Olófin (a manifestation of the Supreme Being) is not present in the igbodún. Remember, Odun was considered so crucial that in the 1800s, it led Adechina to risk his life to return to Africa in order to receive Odun and return to Cuba so babalawos could be initiated on the island. This view regarding the importance of Odun's presence during Ifá initiations are still shared by Yoruba nations such as the Ijebú, Ode Remo, and Ibadan.

The Lucumís have also found themselves being criticized for changes made to ceremonies over the years, such as the receiving of several orichas during the initiation rather than merely receiving Elegguá and their tutelary oricha. The role of obá oriaté, the expert master of ceremonies presiding over the initiation of new santeras or santeros in the Lucumí religion, became a matter of contention, as this position does not exist in Africa.

As I have mentioned, in Nigeria oricha worship consists of hundreds if not thousands of separate religions, and the babalawos are the only priests who work with them all. Neo-traditionalists as well as a number of Yorubas are now propagating the idea of Ifá as the umbrella religion for the disparate oricha cults found there. This becomes similar to the Cuban model, except in place of oriatés and olorichas performing most aspects of oricha initiations, the African model would have the babalawo officiate over each and every one of the rituals in an oricha initiation. In fact, neo-traditionalists have openly stated that if their view were to prevail, the role of the oriaté would cease to exist entirely and their position would be completely usurped by the babalawos who would perform all the rites in the initiation ceremonies for the orichas. As attractive as one might think this would sound to Lucumí babalawos, with all the frictions that have at times transpired between oriatés and babalawos, Lucumí babalawos are vehemently opposed to this. Although the present role of the oriaté may not have existed in Africa, it became an important part of our religion as it evolved in Cuba. Though in the past the babalawos may have performed the work that is now the role of the oriatés, since at least the 1930s the oriatés have been the ones directing initiations.[13, 14] Soon after, the babalawos and the oriatés apparently came to an agreement defining the roles of the oriaté and the babalawo during initiations, and the Lucumí babalawos have honored that agreement ever since.

Though elders of both traditional Lucumí and African forms of the religion generally hold an immense amount of respect for each other, the fact remains that in a number of ways they are now different religions, with different histories and different forms of adapting to the conditions facing them. Two hundred years of separation has led the two traditions to assume different trajectories, but the two traditions have much to learn from each other. In various regions of Yorubaland there are *ese Ifá* (Ifá verses) that are not found in Cuba, and in traditional Ifá form, Lucumí babalawos are eager to add to their knowledge of Ifá. As Awishe Wande Abimbola acknowledges, the Lucumí priests have much to teach the Africans about rituals. In the oddun, Ogbe Di, Ifá predicted that one day our knowledge would be scattered all over the world and that babalawos would have to go to each other to deepen their knowledge. This prophesy of the migration of Ifá fully came to pass as the exodus to the United States served as the springboard for the globalization of the religion that is now being practiced all over the world. Practitioners can be found not only throughout Latin America, particularly in Venezuela and Mexico, but also in France, Austria, England, the Netherlands, and even Russia.

The secrecy of La Santería is still maintained as we are still actively persecuted and discriminated against. This fact was illustrated in 1993 by the landmark case of The Church of the Lukumi Babalu Aye vs. The City of Hialeah contesting laws enacted in Hialeah, and copied by many major cities in the United States denying our religion's right to perform animal sacrifices. The case, brought before the Supreme Court by the church and the ACLU, resulted in a major victory for the Lucumí religion and other religions with similar practices. Although the Lucumí argument prevailed the persecution persists in the United States and elsewhere. In 2009, the practice of animal sacrifice in our religion was back in front of the federal courts in the case of Jose Merced, President Templo Yoruba Omo Orisha Texas, Inc., vs. The City of Euless where the religion once again prevailed against a city determined to end the practice of animal sacrifice. This discriminatory attitude becomes all the more amazing and more than a little ironic when virtually every study you find remarks on how the religion is growing exponentially worldwide. All indications point to a rapid expansion, although the secrecy surrounding the religion prevents an accurate count of how many practitioners there actually are. One conservative estimate found in Migene Gonzáles-Wippler's *Santería: The Religion* is as high as one hundred million in Latin America and the United States alone, although I personally believe that number is a bit high.

Through the hard work and sacrifice of the alagua laguas, who are our most-respected elder babalawos and oricha priests who arrived as slaves, and from a multitude of Yoruba oricha religions, gave birth to one all-inclusive religion that became known as La Regla Ocha, Lucumí, or La Santería. Rather than being a degraded form of Yoruba religion, as some would suggest, the Lucumí religion is its own religion, derived from the Yoruba religions brought to Cuba by Yoruba slaves. On Cuban shores these same African slaves and their direct descendants gave birth to the new Lucumí culture, religion, and identity. The Lucumí tradition or La Regla Ocha (the way of the orichas) is one religion worshipping all of the orichas instead of many religions worshipping each of many orichas, which is perhaps the biggest difference between our African brethren and us. The priest of Changó, of Ochún, of Yemayá, of Obatalá, of Ifá, the babalawo, and the obá oriaté can all say, "We are Lucumí!" The Lucumís have withstood the greatest of hardships and not only survived, but have thrived. Holding to the principles and means by which the alagua laguas used to ensure the survival of the culture, together the Lucumís have the numbers and the power to thrive and grow for generations to come.

The new religion that was given birth to is uniquely Cuban, but its African roots quickly become apparent to anyone who finds themselves at a Lucumí ceremony with its African-derived songs, dances, chants, and prayers. The Lucumi religion is mostly Yoruba, but it is the Yoruba of Adechina, Adé Bí, Efunché, Latuán, and Obatero, and it is their genius and courage that we follow. From Africa to the hostile land that was Cuba they brought the orichas inside themselves, sometimes literally, and transformed it into the religion it is today. That religion has not only survived, but it has thrived and become a world religion.

At the beginning of virtually every ritual is the moyuba. The moyuba means "I salute you," and that's exactly what it is. It usually begins with saluting Olófin and soon carries over to saluting our egguns, all the babalawos in our Ifá line, all the olorichas in our line in Ocha, and all the members of our family who are ibae. This is followed by identifying ourselves by our birth name, our oddun, our name in Ifá, and our name in Ocha. The moyuba tells the orichas who we are and where we came from, because where we came from *is* who we are. The prayer continues with "Emí awó ni Orula (I am a priest of Orula)." Once initiated, this is the other part of who we are: we are Lucumí. Our language, our culture, our songs, our prayers, the way we dress, everything we do in our lives is Lucumí. It is who and what we are.

> *Somos babalawos … Jurado para ayudar la humanidad.*
> *Somos babalawos Ifareando en la Habana donde se Ifarea al duro,*
> *sin guantes.*
> *Somos babalawos …*

> *We are babalawos … Sworn to aid humanity.*
> *We are babalawos … Working Ifá in Havana, where they work Ifá*
> *the hard way, without gloves.*
> *We are babalawos …*

Chapter Six
Orichas and Powers

One day Olófin gave the command that there would be peace on earth, and so all was calm in the world—for a time.

Eventually Obatalá Ayáguna noticed that Olófin wasn't paying attention. Although Obatalá is the oricha of peace and tranquility, Ayáguna is the manifestation of Obatalá at his most fierce and warlike. Ayáguna didn't enjoy disobeying Olófin, but he was too enamored of the warrior life to quit.

One day, Obatalá Ayáguna was waging a particularly bloody battle, cutting off heads left and right with his machete, when suddenly Olófin appeared. Having heard rumors of war, he decided to visit the earth without warning to see if the rumors were true.

When Ayáguna saw Olófin, he quickly wiped his machete across his chest to hide the blood from Olófin. To this day, Obatalá Ayáguna always wears a red sash.

"War will not come to the world if Ayáguna does not give the order."

The orichas are the gods and goddesses ruling over forces of nature as well as human endeavors. They are also the manifestations of the different aspects of Olófin, who divided many of the powers among each of the orichas. In Yorubaland there are hundreds, if not thousands, of orichas, with some not worshipped or even known outside of the city or town where they are located. While many of the orichas were created directly by Olófin, a few were once human beings who, due to their great acts on earth, rose to the level of oricha upon death. One of the meanings of the saying *"Ikú bi oricha* (death gives birth to the oricha)" refers to those who became orichas.

However, there are other forces as well. There are the irunmole (forces), who have power much like the orichas but are often more unpredictable and even dangerous. The irunmole includes the orichas and also such forces as ikú and arun. Among traditional Lucumí practitioners, sometimes the gods and goddesses are divided between those who speak through the diloggún, called ochas, and those who speak exclusively through Ifá, referred to as orichas. Then there are what we refer to as powers. These are forces that are considered greater than orichas but less than Olodumare. Ochas are prepared and given exclusively by santeros, while the orichas and Powers are fabricated and given exclusively by the babalawos. There is an exception to this rule: Odudua, or Oddua, who should be prepared by iworos and babalawos working together. During the preparation of Odudua, the iworos and babalawos often work in the same room, separated only by a white sheet.

Of course, the more powerful something is, the more potentially dangerous it is likely to be. This is true whether we are talking about orichas and powers or mundane forces such as nuclear energy or the electrical outlet in your home. Nuclear energy is extremely powerful, powering the sun and stars, but without the proper precautions being taken, the results can be devastating. The same applies to the orichas and powers. That's why we say "you don't play with the orichas," as one takes them lightly at their own peril. Even sweet orichas like Yemayá and Ochún have dangerous sides. Yemayá may be the all-loving Mother, but she is also responsible for sinking the Titanic. The beautiful, coquettish Ochún is loved but also greatly feared. Some say it's better when she cries than when she laughs, because when she laughs we don't know whether she is truly happy or angry and about to strike and perhaps kill. The deadly flash flood is also Ochún, and in her path of Ibú Ikolé she is considered the queen of the dark witches. Finally, we see that even Obatalá, the oricha of peace and the mind, has a side to him that is anything but peaceful.

The path of Obatalá, known as Ayáguna, is far from peaceful and contemplative, which is Obatalá's stereotype, and is a powerful warrior rivaling Changó who has a love for fomenting revolution.

When a person receives an oricha, they are usually received in the form of stones, nuts, or a container with a carga, or load, such as the load that is placed in Echu Elegguá's cement head. It may be hard to grasp that this is an oricha and a living being, not merely a representation like a statue, but just as you and I inhabit our flesh and bone bodies, the orichas are born through ceremonies and brought down to inhabit these stones and ekines. We are then able to care for the orichas in our own homes by feeding them, communicating with them, and so on. Over time we get to know and love our orichas as we build and deepen our relationships with them.

There are two ways to receive orichas. Adimú orichas, which are received without actually becoming a priest, and those that are received as part of the initiation as an oricha priest or a babalawo. Although adimú orichas need to be taken care of for life, they don't need anywhere near the kind of kind of commitment that becoming a priest requires.

Echu Elegguá

When the world was still young, Echu Elegguá cured Olófin of a grave illness. Olófin asked Elegguá what he wanted in return. Echu, who had suffered hunger and mistreatment in his life, responded, "I wish to always be the first to eat and to live at the door so I will always be saluted first."

Olófin, remembering the circumstances of Echu's birth, smiled and responded, "So it shall be my son. Being the youngest and smallest, you will also be my messenger and the greatest on earth and in heaven, and without your approval it will never be possible for anyone, human or oricha, to do anything. To iban, Echu."

"Echu turns right into wrong, wrong into right."

With one word, Olófin made Echu immensely powerful—perhaps the most powerful oricha of all. Echu is the owner of all roads and doors in life, and he is the gatekeeper of all aché that created the universe, and he holds the key to the particular aché of each of the orichas. Echu is the gatekeeper standing at the crossroads between the two worlds and he is the messenger entrusted by Olófin and Orula to deliver ebbós to the other world.

He is also extremely unpredictable and complex, making him the most misunderstood of all the orichas. Echu stands at the crossroads of all things—between this world and the other, between good and evil, between light and dark—and offerings are often placed at a crossroads for him. Echu is also an oricha of contradictions; he is young and old, big and small, and good and evil all at the same time. In the odduns he is often seen turning great misfortune into even greater fortune and vice versa. Because of his ability to bring about great misfortune, often through trickery, he is often mistakenly associated with the devil by outsiders.

Echu is the divine enforcer for Olófin and for Orula, and he is the oricha they send to deliver their rewards or their punishments. Echu is everywhere and sees everything, making him invaluable to Orula. In addition, Echu is the form in which Ifá explicitly acknowledges the huge role that randomness, chance, and the unforeseeable play in our lives. Many people dread Echu because the unforeseen can be disastrous and because of his fame for causing incalculable confusion and destruction. He is also well-known for his ability to change the appearances of things so that we are tempted into making bad choices based on those appearances. Some give Echu offerings simply in hopes that he won't bring ruin into their lives or what they are attempting to accomplish. Chance and the unforeseen can also work in our favor, and Echu is capable of bringing about great good into our lives and changing the worst situation into the best. As unpredictable as he is, Echu is indispensable because without his aid and permission, nothing can come to pass for humans or orichas, and as dangerous as Echu can be, he can also be the most miraculous.

When Orula came to this world, Olófin gave him Echu Elegguá to accompany and aid him, and they have been inseparable ever since. In his infinite wisdom, Orula made Echu his closest personal assistant, and over time he also became Orula's closest friend. Orula is the only oricha who can keep Echu's more dangerous tendencies under control, which is why he can only be received in full from a babalawo.

One of the greatest mysteries regarding Echu and Ifá was touched upon at a ceremonial dinner in the 1950s when Bernadito Rojas posed a deeply profound observation, "We don't know whether Elegguá is Orula or Orula is Elegguá." His father then countered with an even deeper mystery in response: "We don't know if Orula is Olófin or Olófin is Orula." Thus, the two generations of babalawos pointed to the great mystery that is the continuum between Echu, Orula, and Olófin.[1]

During any ceremony, Echu is the oricha that is saluted first, and he is always given the first offerings. Ceremonies are then closed with the words *"to iban Echu* (it is sealed, with reverence, to Echu)."

Since Echu personifies the immense role randomness plays in our lives, he plays a huge role in Ifá. He is the implicit randomness that makes divination work, and as Orula's messenger he is responsible for causing the correct oddun to appear out of the 256 possibilities present each time Ifá is consulted. Also, as Orula's faithful assistant, Echu can make the unforeseeable work to our advantage and can make even the worst situation end well. Having randomness and the unforeseeable on our side gives us a tremendous edge in life. In Ifá, Echu has many paths, as every oricha has their own paths of Echu who accompany them, and each of the 256 odduns in Ifá has their own Echus. Even our own orí has its own Echu, called Echu n'Ipako.

I am often asked what is the difference between the Echu given by a babalawo and the Elegguá given by a santero. A lot of the confusion comes from the words themselves because Elegguá (or Elegba) is actually one of Echú's titles, and we often refer to Echu as Elegguá or as Echu Elegguá. In practice, the title Echu is most often used to describe him at his full range of power, which includes him at his most dangerous and unpredictable. There are other differences as well. The Echu a babalawo gives contains a number of ingredients, depending on the particular *camino* (path) of Echu being given. Each of the hundreds of paths of Echu is made differently and carries a different carga as well as odduns that have been activated and empowered, and each path of Echu has different characteristics and specialties. Without the intervention of Ifá, Echu is simply too powerful and dangerous for a person to receive, much less bring into their home. Since the Echu prepared by the babalawo is much too powerful and dangerous to put to someone's head, an Elegguá must be prepared by iworos for the initiation of a new santero. The santero's Elegguá can be thought of as an Echu Lite—calm enough to be suitable for putting to a person's head. These Elegguás given by the santeros are a subset of Echu, which are all fashioned in essentially the same way, consisting of a specially consecrated stone. The name of that Elegguá is not revealed until the third day of their initiation as a santero if that is their path in life. We also never refer to the santero's Elegguá as Echu except when we are referring to the name of the particular path of Elegguá. Some santeros refuse to have anything to do with the Echus prepared by babalawos out of fear of Echu's immense power and ability to wreak havoc when angered.

May Echu always open our roads for us and guard them well.
To iban Echu.

The Guerreros: Echu Elegguá, Oggún, Ochossi, and Osun

Orunmila

One day Obatalá wanted to test Orunmila to see if he really had the wisdom to be the advisor to Olodumare and all the orichas. After all, Orula was a very young oricha.

He went to Orula and asked him to make the best food in the world to serve him and his children. Orula agreed and went to the market and bought all the ingredients for the dinner. After cooking all day, he served the dinner to Obatalá and his children, who were truly enchanted with the meal. When the father of the orichas asked Orunmila what he had served, Orunmila replied that it was tongue.

"Why is that?" Obatalá inquired.

"Because with the tongue you can say everything good, and besides it is with the tongue that you give aché," responded Orula.

"I see."

The next day Obatalá asked Orunmila to cook the absolute worst food in the world. Again, Orula agreed and headed off to the market. That night the response of the diners was far different. They were all grumbling and spitting the food out of their mouths. When the meal was done, Obatalá asked Orula what he had cooked that was so awful, to which Orunmila replied, "Tongue."

Surprised, Obatalá said to Orula, "I see. And what did we have last night for the best food in the world?"

"Tongue."

"And why is that?"

"Because with a bad tongue you can disgrace yourself, and with a word you can start a war and bring down a nation. And with a good tongue you can save humanity."

With that, Obatalá gave his approval, and Orula was made advisor to Olodumare and all the orichas.

Orunmila, often shortened to simply Orula, is the oricha of wisdom, knowledge, and divination. He was given the title Elerí Ikúin because he is the only oricha who knows all destinies including those of every human being, the orichas, and the universe. His name means "only the other world knows who will be saved," referring to his role of divining and saving as well as his knowledge of the destiny of everything that exists coming from his direct connection to Olófin. As the oricha of Ifá and divination, Orunmila knows everything, whether it is in the past, present, or future. Orula is the omniscience of Olodumare. Also known as Ifá, he is the system of divination personified. In the oddun Ogbe Funfunló Orula heals a broken world, but the world is perpetually breaking just as Orula is perpetually healing it again.

Osun

Olófin's babalawos habitually got together to hold councils to solicit from Olófin all the things they needed to best perform their tasks as administrators on earth. At one of these councils, Olófin asked what they needed most, already knowing that they had a lot of enemies in the world who constantly attacked them with black magic. All of them sat there not knowing what to say and then started to say many things, but they could not manage to fully comprehend the true scope of what Olófin was asking them.

When it was Ika Roso's turn to speak, he began to outline that what they needed was someone to warn them of any abnormalities when they appeared on earth.

Olófin's interest was piqued. "Just what would this thing that you suggest be like?"

Ika Roso replied, "Osun could warn us of anything abnormal coming."

Olófin smiled and responded, "To iban Echu," and from that day forward, thanks to Ika Roso, the babalawos have Osun.

Osun is the messenger of Olófin and Orula, and when received with the warriors is a short staff with a bird and bells hanging from the cup holding the secret ingredients on top. This staff of Ifá protects your life, your health, and your luck, and it is your first line of defense. In the 1980s, Ifá songs used by babalawos to praise Osun in Ijebuland were found to be identical to those used in Cuba.

Osun has a stand and is kept in a high spot in the home. If Osun falls, it should be taken very seriously. The owner should immediately go to their babalawo godfather so Osun can be fed and have their situation investigated through Ifá to ascertain the nature of the threat and what measures are necessary to protect the life and health of the person. As Lydia Cabrera notes in her book *El Monte*, a few santeros began constructing their own versions of Osun in the 1950s, but these Osuns are hardly traditional since Osun is an oricha who resides squarely in the realm of Ifá.

Osain/Osayín

Osain was a powerful and fearsome sorcerer who lived alone in the wilderness and knew the deepest and darkest secrets to all the plants living there. He jealously guarded his knowledge, and the powers he had gained in the wilderness made him extremely dangerous.

One day Osain decided to go to war against Orula, and before long Osain made life impossible for him. Finally sick of suffering, Orula decided to see what could be done. He saw himself with Ifá, and it was revealed that a fearsome sorcerer had gone to war against him. He needed to make an ebbó to Changó with twelve oil lamps and twelve odduara, or thunder stones, sacred to the oricha of fire for his aid in the upcoming battle.

While Orula was making the ebbó, Osain was gathering his most powerful herbs in order to finish off Orula once and for all. Orula lit the lamps, and as soon as he began the accompanying invocation from the oddun, a huge lightning bolt struck the wilderness where Osain was searching for plants, starting a huge inferno.

Osain soon found himself trapped and surrounded on all sides by the inferno. The screams could be heard all through the forest as the flames consumed Osain, leaving him horribly disfigured with only one arm, one leg, and one eye. Soon after, Orula heard plaintive sobs and whining, and when he went to investigate he saw the horribly burnt Osain. At that moment he knew who his enemy had been all along. Then and there he demanded Osain must serve Ifá, share his secrets with him, and give him permission to use all the plants of the forest. Osain immediately agreed, and since then Osain has worked closely with Ifá.

Osain is the oricha of plants and their magic. He carries within him all the secrets of the wilderness and the powerful magic found there. Osain is indispensable in Ifá and Lucumí religion in general because virtually everything sacred in the religion has been washed in *omiero*, the powerful and sacred lustral liquid made from the plants belonging to Ifá and the orichas.

The Osain received from babalawos is very similar to Palo Monte's *prenda* or *nganga*, the containers that serve as the foundation of the *palero's* (priest) magic and is sometimes called the babalawo's prenda. Like the palero's nganga, the Osain contains special plants, animals, dirts, and bones. It is the babalawo's defense against powerful witchcraft such as that used by paleros, who work the negative side of their religion.[2] The containers housing Osain's secrets can take several shapes depending on what Ifá calls for during divination.

Babalawos use their Osains when they need to go to war for themselves, for their godchildren, or for their clients. Because Osain is the owner of all the *palos* (sticks), it is not surprising that their construction is very similar to the palero's nganga and can be used for positive or negative works when necessary.

Babalawos also prepare amulets, called oniche Osains, that are used to defend a client or bring them good fortune. Some are also prepared for the orichas to strengthen them and to use as tools. Women are not allowed to receive Osain in any form until after they have stopped menstruating, for the protection of the woman's health.

Olokun

When Olófin commanded that children be made in the world, Olokun sent down his daughter Aje, who was very ugly but had all the riches in the world. When he arrived, Olokun turned her over to a group of men who lived on the seashore, but they simply ignored her and went on their way, forgetting about Olokun and his daughter. Annoyed, Olokun went in search of the men, and the same waves that had announced riches now announced death and destruction.

Orunmila was very poor, and Eleggua went to visit him. Afterward, they went to a secret location to take a look at Olokun's riches. Orunmila wanted to pick the most beautiful items, and Echu advised him that he could choose all he wanted but could not take anything. Aje passed by and told him to pick one, so Orula did.

Echu turned to Orunmila and said, "You have ruined me!" All the riches were pulled into the sea, and now they were both penniless.

Meanwhile, Echu left Orunmila's side and went to Olokun's house. When the riches returned to the depths of the sea, Olokun wondered why they had come back. Then it hit him "Where was Aje!?"

Echu said to Olokun, "Don't worry. She's at Orunmila's house and she's just fine." The news pleased Olokun to no end, and he decided he would reward Orula handsomely. From that instant, Orunmila was astoundingly rich and had many healthy, strong children, thanks to Olokun.

Olokun, whose name simply means "owner of the sea," is not properly a Yoruba deity but instead hails from Edo people in the kingdom of Benin. He is the owner of the depths of the sea and is an exceptionally powerful and mysterious oricha. Incalculably rich, he lives surrounded by the dead in the darkest depths of the ocean. He is unknown and unknowable and is the keeper of unfathomable secrets. Over the years Olokun became incorporated into the Yoruba pantheon and traveled to Cuba with both Edo and Yoruba slaves. The crocodile, the python, and the manatee are Olokun's most sacred animals, and to this day, on occasion, a crocodile is sacrificed to the oricha by babalawos in Cuba in order to gain Olokun's blessings and protection.

Olokun can be received from a babalawo or an iworo, but the Olokun that the santeros give is a path of Yemayá called Mayelewo (Agana Erí in the Matanzas area) who is extremely close to Olokun and has a deep rapport with him. Physically the two types of Olokun are quite different. The Olokun de santero lives in a terra cotta or ceramic pot that is filled with water. On the other hand, the Olokun de babalawo lives in a pot covered in seashells and is accompanied by members of Olokun's royal court, each in their own tiny pot that hangs from the larger pot. Also the Olokun de babalawo comes with his own Echu. The ceremony for receiving this Olokun is also much more involved and intense, and includes a full itá where Olokun gives his advice through an oddun that accompanies the initiate for life. This itá is performed using the Table of Ifá with four babalawos present to interpret the oddluns that are revealed. The santero's Olokun is much simpler;

being composed much like any oricha received from a santero. Two of the greatest differences between the two are when one receives an Olokun de santero. There is no itá received with an Olokun received from a santero, and the Olokun de santero must always be kept full of water, whereas the Olokun born in Ifá has an itá and is kept dry or almost dry. This does not mean that the Olokun de santero is not effective, for it most certainly is, and some feel the added expense and effort in receiving the babalawo Olokun is not necessary.

There is a ceremony where Olokun is fed at a deep spot in the sea, but it is extremely dangerous. There used to be a ceremony in Cuba where Olokun was fed at sea, followed by the dancing of Olokun's masks to the rhythms of Olokun's special drums. Each time this ceremony was performed, a babalawo was expected to die as a result. This ceremony ceased being observed after Tata Gaitán died soon after performing the ceremony in 1944.

Oddua/Oduduwa

In the earliest days of putting the world in order, Orunmila and Oddua were two brothers who were exceptionally close and lived in Ifé, where they were experiencing a lot of misery. One day they decided they would travel to other lands to see if they could find something to help Ifé. They also decided that each would leave their daughter with the other. Orunmila brought Poroyé and Oduduwa brought Aloshé, both daughters of Ochún. After passing through many lands they came to a forest. Orunmila and his daughter began to feel hungry, but since they had no food Oduduwa said, "Take care of Aloshé so I can go out and try to find something to hunt."

But Oduduwa couldn't find anything to hunt so he said to himself, "I can't let my beloved brother and his daughter suffer from hunger." He then grabbed his tongue and with a knife cut off a big chunk of his tongue. He then dumped a little iyefá in his mouth, lit a fire, and cooked his tongue covered with herbs and brought them to Orunmila so that he and his daughter could eat.

As Orunmila was so hungry, he decided it must have been a miracle from Olófin.

Afterward, Oduduwa stuffed a piece of coconut in his mouth and was able to speak perfectly! Then they continued on their journey until they came to a very arid spot, but Oduduwa was losing blood fast and fatigue was debilitating him, so he had to tell Orunmila, "My brother, I am injured and have lost a lot of blood, so you take the road and keep checking the Niger River. When I feel better, I will catch up with you."

"Let me see the wound; perhaps I can cure it." At seeing what was once his brother's tongue, Orunmila suddenly understood his sacrifice and began to cry inconsolably. Orunmila then went into action. He grabbed a piece of coconut and whittled it down to the same size and shape as the old one. He then sat and marked a number of odduns to cure his brother, activated them with their prayers, and stuffed the iyefá into Oduduwa's mouth. Soon the bleeding stopped and they went to the Niger River together.

There Orunmila turned to his brother and said, "Since your tongue is now made out of coconut, I will speak for you and for me. I am going to go far and find my fortune. I will leave my daughter Poroye with you to take care of." And, grabbing his ecuele, he was off in an instant.

As time passed, Oduduwa began to hear of his brother Orunmila's fame as a diviner and was very happy for this, but as it turns out one day Poroye became gravely ill and died. Oduduwa, despairing from the events facing him, cried out, "Oh, how great is my pain! Well then, my daughter will also die so that my pain will accompany him." Seizing a knife, he killed his very own daughter. Oduduwa then set about making a great tomb on the west side of a ceiba tree and buried the two daughters, crying bitterly the entire time.

The very next day Orunmila came to visit. Shocked by Oduduwa's mood, he began to ask about his daughter Poroye—almost before saluting his brother.

Oduduwa's words came pouring out of him. "Oh, my brother! What a great pain I feel! Yesterday your daughter died of an unknown disease, and I ... thinking about the pain you would feel when you would be informed about this ... I killed my own daughter to accompany her so I could suffer just the same as you."

Orunmila responded, "Take me to where they are buried." Upon arriving, Orunmila said to Oduduwa, "Do you agree how powerful we are when we bond together?" Oduduwa nodded solemnly.

"Now let us call our brother Orun, Ikú's husband." Orunmila prepared his Table of Ifá and Oduduwa his agogó bells and they both called Orun, who appeared immediately and asked the brothers what they wished.

They replied in unison, "We need you to return our daughters to life."

Orun then responded, "Okay, then. You will have to do this and this and this and this ..." (Nobody but Orun, Orula, and Oduduwa know exactly what was done to bring the two girls back to life.)

When they opened the grave back up, both of their daughters were alive! Whereupon Orunmila and Oduduwa made a pact to always have mutual respect and never do anything to harm the other, and to seal the pact they made a special teja marked with odduns on it.

From that day forward, they have respected each other and been united, and that is why Oduduwa only speaks through Ifá.

Oduduwa, also known as Oddua, is the oricha who presides over the secrets of life and death and rules the line between the two. Oddua often manifests as a formless, spiritual mass of enormous power that lives in the deepest, darkest shadows of the night. Oduduwa is one of the greatest mysteries we have. Oddua is responsible for creating the first land out of the waters that covered the early world when Obatalá, who was originally sent by Olófin to do the job, drank too much palm wine and fell asleep. The first land created was Ilé Ifé itself.

A lot of confusion surrounds Oduduwa as the human founder of the city–state of Ifé and of the Yoruba people who had the same name, which has caused many people to mix the two over time. Others have concluded that they are one and the same, and that Oduduwa is a deified ancestor. Every year in Ilé Ifé, the Ooni's ekin nuts for Oduduwa are fed as part of Orunmila's yearly festival.

Olófin/Odun—God in My Closet

One day Odun decided to come to the world to visit Orunmila, but the form she took upon arrival was very, very strange. Her skin was extremely pale, almost translucent; she had no arms or legs, and she was nearly blind. In fact, she appeared more like an albino snake than a woman.

When she arrived on earth, the first women she encountered teased her mercilessly for her looks. There were no bounds to the cruelty they heaped upon what they thought was a helpless cripple. Little did they know about the terrible and wonderful power hidden within her—a power allowing anything she said to come to pass; with a word she could make a planet blow up or give birth to a new star. Their actions hurt Odun deeply and instilled in her a terrible impression of women that would lead to consequences lasting to this very day.

Meanwhile, Orunmila was being seen with Ifá by two babalawos. One was named If You Teach Someone to Be Intelligent, They Will Become Truly Intelligent and the other babalawo's name was If You Teach Someone To Be Stupid, They Will Become Truly Stupid. They told Orunmila a woman was arriving with a terrible power in her hands. They told him he should make her his wife but he must first make ebbó quickly so Odun would not kill the people of earth out of anger. Orunmila immediately made an ebbó, and when Odun arrived, eating the ebbó calmed her. This was truly fortunate, as the women had angered her so much she was on the verge of killing everyone on earth.

She asked, "Who made this ebbó with all my favorite foods?"

Echu responded, "It was Orunmila. He wishes to marry you."

Odun responded with a faint smile, "Not bad. He knows me." Odun arrived at Orunmila's home to tell him that she would marry him.

"I have many, many powers. I will fight your battles for you and I will never let you suffer, but there are conditions that you must meet. First I must live in a round house without light because the light hurts my sensitive eyes. And you must never allow any woman to look upon me or be in my presence."

She told Orula that if he agreed to all her conditions she would protect him from all harm, she would bestow all kinds of good on him, and she would share the secrets of her immense power with him. She would change his burdens into blessings, and if anyone tried to harm him she would annihilate them completely. Finally, she gave Orunmila a stern warning: "Do not trifle with me. Do not let your children, the babalawos, trifle with me. I am not to be played with."

She continued, "Without my presence at initiation, that person does not have Ifá and may not divine with Ifá. And a babalawo will finally be complete when he receives me. To iban Echu."

Orula immediately agreed, and Odun became his most important wife and the true source of his power—and, in turn, the power of his priests, the babalawos.

Olófin is the Creator of everything in the universe.[3] Although extremely remote, Olófin is considered the least distant of the three manifestations of the Supreme Being in our tradition. Olófin is also known as Odun, and as such, she is considered by many to be the wife of Olodumare. Their relationship is sometimes depicted as two calabashes sealing and containing the universe. Many consider Olófin to be just another title of Olodumare, and that the Olófin/Odun received in Cuba actually contains both genders, and what babalawos receive in Cuba is that closed calabash of Olodumare (Olófin) and Odun.

Odun is the mother of all the odduns that make up Ifá and the universe as the ultimate source of the babalawos' power, which is why Odun is sometimes referred to as *Igba Iwá Odun* (Odun, the calabash of all existence). The only way a person can work with odduns is through her, which is why her presence is indispensable for the initiation of an Ifá priest in Afro-Cuban Ifá, as well as in the areas of Yorubaland, which haven't lost this secret. Besides the pataki above, there is another oddun where Ifá flatly states that anyone who attempts to be initiated without her *igba* (receptacle) present will accomplish nothing and Orula will not recognize that person as his priest. As explained earlier, Odun was so crucial for Ifá initiations that Adechina was willing to risk life and limb to return to Africa, receive her, and smuggle her back into Cuba so Ifá might survive on the island. The pataki above also illustrates how dangerous Odun can be when she is angered. She can blind or kill those who trifle with her in any way. Olófin should only be received by babalawos who are elder in years and knowledge and have proven themselves to be worthy of this tremendous responsibility.

Olófin is physically received by very few babalawos chosen by Ifá who show their elders they are experienced and have good character. They are then known as Olofistas or omo Odun, and make up the highest grade of babalawos. Those babalawos with whom she lives with must follow strict rules regarding how she is cared for. She must be kept in her own area, usually a small, dark, specially prepared room or closet, locked away from the prying eyes of the uninitiated.

Orí Eledá

Once there was a man who was always asking for help from the orichas and his Orí but never gave anything in return. One day the man went to be seen with Ifá and was told to make ebbó to avoid being taken from the world, but he refused. Not long after, his Orí came for him and began to unceremoniously drag him, kicking and screaming, from his house by his feet.

As they passed Ogún's house, he screamed for help. "Ogún, save me!" But Ogún, seeing that it was Orí dragging him away, merely shrugged his shoulders, as he could do nothing to help. As they passed Changó's house, he screamed for help again, but Changó couldn't help him either. This happened with each of the orichas, and none of them could do anything to help.

Finally, as they passed by Orula's house, the man cried out one last time. Orula came out and asked Orí whether he would release the man if he could guarantee he would make the necessary offerings. Orí hesitated, for he was extremely angry, but finally relented and agreed. And from then on, the man always made his offerings on time.

Orí (also Erí or Lerí) literally means head, but in Ifá it is much more than just the container we keep our brain in. Often referred to as Orí Eledá, or Orí the creator, your orí is your own personal creator who creates and rules over every aspect of your life. This includes your talents, your personality, everything you are, and everything you are going to be. One's orí is a piece of Olodumare that resides in each of us.

Even more, your orí is an exceptionally powerful deity in its own right. More powerful than the orichas themselves, as we saw in the pataki above, your orí can affect every part of your being, including your health, your luck, and the way your life unfolds. In another pataki, the orí is responsible for giving the orichas their roles and placing them on earth. Your orí is your spiritual DNA, so to speak, and for those whose destinies include becoming initiated as olorichas, the initiation fuses their orí with their tutelary oricha that accompanies them to this world, allowing them to attain greater balance, alignment, and power.

We all have a spirit double who lives in the other world as well. This is our orí in its purest form, and the more we are attuned to this undiluted version of ourselves, the greater and more fulfilled we become. Offerings made to your orí, usually made in the form of the ritual known as keborí eledá, are shared with your double in the other world.

There is another manifestation of orí that resides wholly in Orun, the other world. Known as orí acueré, it is the archetype from which all orís are born. This quintessential orí rules over and controls the destinies of everything that has an orí, whether it be a bird, a human being, an oricha, or Odun herself. Everything in the universe has a destiny and orí rules over them all.

In Africa it used to be that only elder babalawos and kings were allowed to receive Orí Acueré. This should not be confused with the orí often seen in Africa consisting of a leather cone with sand that has had the oddun Ofún Bile marked in it and forty-one cowries attached to it. This is a shrine to our Orí inú, or personal orí, and not Orí Acueré. It is unknown if they still have the older one in Yorubaland, but in Cuba this deified archetypal Orí Acueré can only be received by elder babalawos who have already received Olófin/Odun, illustrating Orí's immense importance in Afro-Cuban Ifá.

One way of understanding this is to consider your personal orí as your individual consciousness, and the archetypal Orí Acueré as a kind of Cosmic or Absolute Consciousness from which all consciousness emanates and spans the universe. It is possible for a person whose personal orí is fully in alignment with Orí Acueré to apprehend the information constituting the universe directly. From there the person can direct their consciousness, allowing them to play a much bigger part in the day to day creation of the universe around them. Or, as Ifá tells us in the refrán from the oddun Baba Eyiogbe, "Wisdom, understanding, and thought are the forces that move the world."

Chapter Seven
Initiations

When the world was still very young Orula was sent to earth in search of a land called Ilé Ifé, the spiritual capital of the world, where he was to teach Ifá and the proper way to live to the people who lived there. When Orula came to the world with his Ifá, he arrived at a place called Onika, which was on the shores of the sea. Leading out from Onika were sixteen roads, and Orula patiently began taking each road to its end, one at a time. Each road was more difficult than the last, and on his travels he encountered all the peoples of the world, but none of the roads led to Ilé Ifé.

There was finally only one road left, a desolate path leading straight into the shifting sands of the desert. Orula followed this last road until he was stumbling blind through the sand, his clothes in tatters, and with no food or water. As he was about to give up out of despair, through clouded eyes he thought he spied a tiny oasis with a small pool of water and somehow managed to crawl his way over to it.

When he arrived at the oasis, he found three sacred trees. An iroko, an araba, and a palm tree were growing next to the spring. Orula was delirious as he cried out to Olófin that he had failed his quest to find the sacred city of Ilé Ifé and that he was tired of the endless traveling and hardship.

Suddenly Orula heard a thunderous voice saying, "The more you look, the less you see. You do not even see what is right in front of your own nose."

The voice then ordered Orula to take his Ifá in his hands, submerge the ekin nuts in the spring, and throw the water into his eyes and over his back. As he did so, he heard singing. "Alagba nfo gede...oju, alagba nfo gede...ofo." [1] *When he looked up his eyes were clear, and just in front of him was the entrance to Ilé Ifé.*

And from that day forward that spring with its three sacred trees became the first Igbodún for the initiation of new babalawos.

"The best way to know nothing is to try to learn everything at once."

At OrishaNet.org I am asked more questions regarding initiations than all of the other subjects combined, with at least three quarters of the e-mails I receive being about initiations. Often enough they are straightforward requests to be initiated, but important questions regarding initiation also come in on a regular basis. How do I know if this is the right path for me? What kind of commitment will be expected of me? What steps do I need to take to get initiated?

Is Santería the Right Path for Me?

The first piece of advice I can give is unless there is a real emergency, take your time to learn about the religion to see if it's right for you. Santería is an exceptionally serious religion requiring serious commitment with serious amounts of work involved, especially in the higher levels of initiation. As santeros and babalawos we live our religion twenty-four hours a day seven days a week. Even what, when, where or how we eat, sleep or even make love can be affected by what the orichas ask of us. You should also take your time in choosing your godparents, the priests whom you will be entrusting with your spiritual well-being and advancement. Are they serious about the religion themselves? Are they honest and helpful toward their godchildren? And, although priests in our religion often lead extremely busy lives, your *madrina* (godmother) or padrino should be willing to give you a reasonable amount of their time and it should not be entirely about money. Santeros and babalawos have to eat too and should be paid decently for the work they do, but if you can't get even a moment of their time without money being involved you might want to think twice before making what should be a lifetime commitment with them.

On the subject of money, the would-be initiate should know that they are not buying an oricha or an initiation. The *derecho* (money) they pay for the initiation is ritual payment for the actual work being done and the materials needed for the initiation. Many initiations require an immeasurable amount of work from multiple highly trained priests, and that costs money and it is only right that the initiate pay for this labor. This is accompanied by the sad fact that most people in our society will not appreciate an initiation unless the cost makes it dear to them.

The Orichas Make the Final Decision

Whether someone is to be initiated at any level in Santería is up to Ifá and the orichas. Most of the time the way a person finds out is when it comes up during a consultation with Ifá or with the shells that a person needs to receive one or more initiations. An oricha can also come down and possess one of their priests who tell you that you need to receive an initiation. One may also be told they don't need initiations or that they should not receive certain initiations at all. There are also odduns that may say the person is not suitable for that particular priest for one reason or another.

There are some rules of thumb that can be helpful. If you go to a priest who tells everyone that they need to receive the whole pantheon of orichas and initiations immediately even if everything is going great in their lives, it should pop up some warning flags. While it can happen that the orichas will want you to receive a lot of initiations quickly it is an extremely rare occurrence. In more than twenty years of working as a priest in the religion I have experienced the orichas calling for this only a handful of times. Not everyone is meant to be in the religion, much less become a santero or babalawo.

In my own case, the very first time I was seen with Ifá the oddun that came up was the one where the Table of Ifá was born. In that oddun Ifá said that I needed to become a babalawo, as I was born to be an

Ifá priest, and that I had been practicing Ifá in heaven before coming to this world. But even then my padrino-to-be told me that whether or not I was to become a babalawo had to be confirmed by Ifá directly when I received my abo faca. By confirming everything with Ifá and the orichas every step of the way, we avoid running into problems and can be sure of success. We can also be sure that the orichas will be content with us.

What Kind of Commitment Will Be Expected of Me?

In the beginning initiations, such as receiving the *elekes* (necklaces), the commitment is serious but not terribly onerous. For instance, you are expected to go to your godparents' house on the anniversary of their initiations as priests. On the feast day of their oricha you are to go with a plate, two coconuts, two candles, and a derecho if the godparent is a santero; or a plate, two ñames (Caribbean yams—*Dioscorea rotundata*), two candles, and the derecho if they are a babalawo. You are also expected to go and help with basic chores such as cleaning or plucking chickens any time your godparents have a ceremony. Many times it is while doing these chores that godparents will teach you, and you generally learn a lot from helping them.

When you actually receive an oricha, such as Echu Elegguá and the warriors Oggún, Ochossi, and Osun, you are expected to take care of that oricha for life. Initiation as a santero or babalawo is a very big and lifelong commitment, so the decision on whether or not to be initiated into the priesthood should be taken very seriously. Those who are initiated on a whim and later decided to abandon the orichas risk incurring the wrath of their own orichas, and that does not usually end well. Not everyone is born to be a santero or a babalawo.

How Do I Find an Ilé?

Again, you should take your time choosing the right ilé. Are the godparents close to their orichas? Are they concerned with teaching their godchildren to learn our religion and culture well? In this religion we don't learn through classes or seminars but learn directly from our padrinos. Most of our learning is done while working to help our godparents.

If a babalawo or oloricha is kind enough to invite you to a ceremony you are being offered a great opportunity and should go. Ask what you can bring and what you should wear. This will show them that you are being respectful and serious. In fact, being respectful every step of the way is extremely important. You are dealing with priestesses and priests in a religion and culture based on respect so if you are rude and demanding they will not want to have anything to do with you.

If you receive an initiation and simply wait expecting your madrina or padrino to sit you down and teach you secrets about the orichas without paying your dues and working you will probably do a lot of waiting and very little learning. In fact, initiations only allow us to be in the room during ceremonies for that oricha. From there it is up to us to take the initiative and help our madrinas and padrinos with the hard and dirty work of cleaning, preparing, holding, and any other type of hard work. It is during this time that most padrinos and madrinas teach their godchildren things about the ceremonies and orichas. In my case my early training was with my padrino Guillermo who was very traditional and very tough, and everything I learned was gained through hard work and a lot of patience.

Godparents will have their own style of teaching. Some are easygoing and some are strict like my padrino Guillermo. But for all of us knowledge is something to be earned, not bought, sold, or given away.

Which Initiation Goes First?

In the strictest ilés a person would often receive their guerreros and kofá or abo faca before receiving their elekes.[2] This is because the kofá or abo faca ceremony is typically when a person finds out the identity of their oricha. This way they are sure to receive the necklaces for their oricha. Otherwise the elekes will have to be prepared as if the person is a child of Obatalá, and make any necessary changes once the initiate learns the identity of their oricha. With that being said, once again it is all up to Ifá and the orichas. Sometimes Ifá will say the person needs their elekes first. There are also ilés that give the necklaces first. Neither way is really wrong. It depends on the Ocha house you belong to.

There are initiations like the elekes that are performed solely by the iworos, and the iworos perform the vast majority of the rituals within the initiation of the oricha priest called the kariocha. Because this is a book on Ifá we will focus on the initiations received through Ifá from the hands of the babalawos.

During one's lifetime a person might be called on to receive a number of other orichas through Ifá. For instance, one might need to receive Olokun, the owner of the sea and its depths, and Oddua, the most powerful oricha in Olófin's court who represents both life and death, which we learned about in chapter 6. These immensely powerful orichas are both received with in-depth itás and impart a tremendous amount of aché to our lives.

Guerreros

The guerreros, or warriors, are the fundamental initiation in the religion. Receiving the guerreros is a big step because it formally makes a person part of an ilé with all the attendant responsibilities and obligations. The most obvious is the need to go over to your *oluwo's* (babalawo godfather's) home for the anniversary of his initiation as an Ifá priest and the celebration of Orunmila's birthday.

The babalawo begins the process by performing a special divination with ecuele to find out which camino of Echu accompanies the godchild-to-be out of the more than 250 possible paths of Echu. They also find out what stones or other objects are needed because each path of Echu is constructed differently. Each of the paths of Echu has special strengths, and some of these paths require special care and treatment. Echu is crucial for communication with the orichas, as well as keeping our doors and roads open while closing those that wish to do you harm.[3]

Besides Echu, Oggún, Ochossi, and Osun are also received when the guerreros are prepared by a babalawo. They all live near the front door of the house, except for Osun, who is placed in a high place within the home. Oggún is the oricha of war as well as the blacksmith of the orichas. This is why technology often starts as weapons and only later gets used for more peaceful purposes. Oggún defends us and our homes, and helps us to find work. Ochossi is the oricha of the hunt and uses bows, arrows, and traps to capture his prey. He is also the policeman of the orichas and because of this the police are sometimes referred to as Ochossis. Ochossi also defends us, helps us to avoid traps, and guides us to hunt the good things in life. The warriors are close friends and always travel together which is why they are received as a group.

Twenty-one days after you receive your warriors, you should have an *entrada* (entrance) where your Guerreros are fed at your home. This is the beginning of your reciprocal relationship with your Guerreros and will continue most often with weekly Monday offerings of candle, rum, cigars, and water along with their special prayers. Over time instruction is given as to how to give obí to the warriors to ask them simple yes or no questions.

Iworos also give their own version of the warriors, but there are a couple major differences between the two versions. First, instead of receiving Echu in full the initiate receives an Elegguá whose name and path will be learned if and when they are fully initiated as a santero in the kariocha ceremony. The Echu given by the babalawos cannot be used in the kariocha ceremony because Echu is simply too powerful to be put to someone's head, so an Elegguá must be prepared for the initiation. Second, santeros aren't empowered to give Osun, which is specifically an Ifá staff. Osun watches over the well-being of the initiate and will fall over to warn the initiate of impending danger. Despite the differences the warriors given by santeros are also effective as many people who have received them will attest. The warriors are the first line of defense for initiates and are depended on to fight and win their battles.

One Thanksgiving afternoon a person came to my home three times. Apparently a friend of his had decided that he had been the victim of some sort of witchcraft and that we had been the source. With each visit the person became more agitated and more threatening. On the third visit he resorted to a death threat. I ran to confront him about it, but he had already left.

A couple months later he appeared at our neighborhood supermarket, where I confronted him, but he stomped off. When we went to leave the store I realized the entrance might be a good spot for an ambush. I went ahead and as the automatic doors opened I leapt out to one side to lend an element of surprise to anyone who might be waiting. Fortunately no one was waiting there, but a couple of men who had seen the confrontation had a story to tell.

Apparently the man had indeed intended to ambush us and had gone to his car to retrieve a sword he kept in the trunk, but as he pulled the sword out a burly black man in a van parked next to him said, "What the (blank) do you think you're doing?"

Our wayward neighbor simply responded, "(blank) you."

To this, the man in van pulled out a .357 Magnum and put it right into our would-be attacker's face. With that, our neighbor threw his sword on the seat, jumped into his car, and sped off. From that day forward, whenever he saw us, he would hurriedly cross to the other side of the street to avoid us. Oggún fought our battle for us that day, and we did not have to lift a finger. That is why we say "may Oggún always fight your battles for you" when we give the warriors to a new initiate.

Kofá and Abo faca: The Hand of Orula

The ceremony known as kofá for women and abo faca for men is the fundamental initiation into Ifá. This initiation bestows the Orula's blessings on the person as well as placing them under the wise oricha's protection. During the three-day initiation the initiate receives Orula, who will live in a small porcelain or wooden container, and will receive an extensive itá where their destiny is revealed. The babalawos will close the itá with an inquiry into which oricha is the initiate's *Olorí oricha* (Owner of the Head) or tutelary oricha.

On the last day an *iddé* (bracelet) made of green and yellow beads is put on the person's left wrist in a short ceremony. This bracelet, whose full name is *idefá* (Ifa's iddé), identifies them as one of Orula's children and ikú cannot take them without asking Orula's permission due to the ancient pact Orula made with Death. Not all parts of Africa have this exact ceremony but there are two rituals that are performed every-where for babies to help the child be properly situated in the world. These are *Ikoshe W'aye* (stepping into the world) and *Imorí* (knowing the head). They later receive an initiation known as *ishefá* that is very much the equivalent to the kofá and the abo faca.

Though for the most part the kofá and abo faca ceremonies are very similar, women undergo more ceremonies than their male counter-parts. Women who have received their kofá are known as apetebís and are the caretakers of Orunmila. An apetebí is considered to be elder to the men who have received abo faca, and they are allowed to partici-pate in ceremonies that are closed to abo faca initiates. The apetebí is considered the right hand of the babalawo and are highly respected.

One of the roles of the apetebí is to dance for the babalawos when there is a drumming ceremony for the orichas because babalawos are prohibited from dancing. While the drummers play the songs for Orula the apetebís dance in a circle around the babalawos, and the babalawos put money to each apetebí's head as they pass. This derecho is payment for their work and is used to buy items for the apetebí's oricha or Orula.

When we receive kofá or abo faca besides putting us under the pro-tection and blessings of Orunmila, we are informed of our *itan* (road or destiny). Probably the most important part of the initiation, the itá is a deep divination using the Table of Ifá that is performed by three or more babalawos. Orula, who was given the title Elerí Iküín by Olodu-mare, is the only oricha allowed to witness our destinies being be-stowed upon us. Therefore, Ifá is the only oricha empowered by Olod-umare to reveal that destiny to us. During the itá the true nature of the person is revealed along with in-depth advice on how to best live out our lives. By following Orunmila's advice the person can advance in life and avoid the pitfalls that can happen to most people.

As part of our destiny we are often given a number of ewós pertaining to the oddun that must be followed. These prohibitions are not a punishment but are intended to protect us as with the godchild who was prohibited from eating pork. By revealing our path in life Ifá gives us the means to live out our lives in the most fulfilling way possible. Unfortunately, most of us spend our days undoing ourselves working counter to our own destinies, and only finding problems in life because of it. Our destiny is the story of our lives as it is played out against the backdrop of the universe. Although most of our destinies were written before we were even born, there are many things we can do to better or worsen our fate. This is the meaning of the refrán "Each person is as Obatalá made them, but what we become is up to us."

Each oddun has irés and osogbos, its own good and bad fortunes, that are the consequences of how we live out our destinies. We say that how our lives will end up depends on how we live our oddun in life. A person can do the things that will ensure they mostly receive the irés of their sign or they can act in such a way that will force us to experience mostly the osogbos and their consequences. This is what we call living our irés or living our osogbos. Ultimately our fate is in our hands.

Ocha/Kariocha

Commonly referred to as "Making Ocha" the kariocha is the initiation of a new iworo. Although it is properly in the terrain of the oriatés and santeros, I had to include this ceremony because it can be such a perfect example of how well things work when the oriatés, babalawos, and iworos cooperate in perfect harmony.

It appears that at one point babalawos had a much larger role in the kariocha ceremony than they do now. In some lineages babalawos were in charge of shaving the head of the new initiate and on some occasions even carrying out the itá performed on the third day of the kariocha. On these occasions, even the itá was sometimes performed using the Table of Ifá instead of the orichas' shells. Agreements were later made that defined the roles of the obá oriaté and the babalawo in the ceremony. Although no solid evidence has been found, most people in Cuba believe that some sort of agreement was made between the legendary Tata Gaitán and the seminal oriaté Obadimeyi. The babalawo's role in the ceremony was greatly lessened and is now relatively light with many of the jobs now the responsibility of the oriaté.[4]

Many babalawos still blame Tata Gaitán for making this agreement that lessened the babalawo's role in the kariocha. These babalawos believe this agreement ultimately created a slippery slope allowing certain oriatés to attempt a power play on the babalawos and allowing them to perform ceremonies and initiations that are traditionally part of the babalawos' role. However, all evidence shows that during the time of Tata Gaitán and Obadimeyi only the deepest respect was shown between babalawos and oriatés. It wasn't until long after the deaths of both Tata Gaitán and Obadimeyi that any of these problems began to appear. The fact is, the oriaté has been responsible for most of the kariocha ceremony, with the babalawos only exercising the roles listed above since as far back as the 1930s and this should be respected. The obá oriaté is indispensable in the religion and the depth of their knowledge is worthy of the greatest respect. Their immense knowledge and wisdom make these specialists second only to the babalawos. Babalawos and oriatés are the two summits of the Lucumí religion.

Making Ifá: The Initiation of the Babalawo

The initiation of a babalawo is called making Ifá. The initiation is exceptionally intensive, and like the kariocha initiation of the iworos, lasts for one week. For the ceremony to be considered valid by Orula as well as other babalawos Olófin's canister, also called Igba Iwá Odun or Odun's calabash of all existence, must be in the room. Her presence lends the new initiate her aché and enables them to work with the odduns of Ifá. New babalawos actually begin their training during the week long initiation, a big difference between making Ifá and the kariocha ceremony is that the new santeros must wait at least three months to start learning in earnest.

After this there are two more levels or grades in Ifá. One is *kuanado* that is a ceremony empowering the babalawo to use the knife to sacrifice four-legged animals and allows the babalawo to initiate new babalawos. The second is when a babalawo achieves the highest grade in Ifá upon receiving Olófin or "God's Mysteries." These initiates, commonly called *Olofistas* or omo odun are rare because Olófin is to be given only to those babalawos who are not only very experienced and knowledgeable, but also uphold the very highest ethical standards.

Chapter Eight
Ebbó: Sacrifices and Offerings

One day Olodumare declared a contest between Ebbó and Ogo to see which one was strongest. Olodumare declared that whoever could go one week without food would be declared the winner and would become his close personal assistant.

Everyone expected Ogo to win because he was strong, fast, and often achieved spectacular results. Ogo always worked alone, feeling he didn't need to share his fame or his rewards with anyone. Furthermore, Ogo didn't mind doing all kinds of work no matter how injurious it might be as long as he was well paid.

On the other hand, Ebbó took his time working methodically to ensure everything he did was done correctly so the results would be certain. Ebbó never forgot to give a share to Echu and would often share with the other orichas as well. Ebbó also refused to do any harm to others, an attitude that only furthered the impression that he was weak.

On the first night of the competition Ebbó was already feeling weak when Echu suddenly appeared with food and drink. "You have always shared with me," declared Echu. "Now it's time for me to return the favor."

By the third day Ogo succumbed to his hunger and began to dig through a trash bin in search of scraps to eat. Echu seized Ogo and dragged him before Olodumare, who declared Ebbó the winner of the contest. From that day forward, Echu carries ebbós directly to Olodumare—after Echu takes his share, of course ...

"I can do anything; ebbó is great through the will of Olodumare."

The babalawo sits on the mat, a round hardwood table with sacred symbols engraved on its rim lying between his outstretched legs. This is the Table of Ifá, the babalawos greatest tool, whose inside diameter is covered with the sacred iyefá powder. Set neatly beside him is the rooster and scalpel that will be used in the sacrifice. The babalawo begins to wipe the iyefa dust with a brown paper packet in counter clockwise circles, while tapping the edge of the Table with an *irofa* (tapper) made from a deer antler. He is performing the ebbó katero, one of the most powerful rituals at the babalawo's command. Marked on the Table of Ifá are more than forty odduns. Each has its own special power and job within the ritual. The babalawo must now activate each of the odduns by using the correct prayers and songs learned through countless hours of memorization and practice. With the prayer *"Oché Turá Echu awatetete* (Echu, come quickly)" the Ifá priest begins the seemingly endless litany of prayers and chants.

The spot in front of the Table of Ifá where the client would sit is empty, because this time the client is the babalawo himself. A large tumor had been found in the babalawo's pelvic region and a life threatening surgery has been scheduled for the following week. Today the babalawo must work hard to save his own life through the power of Orula and Ifá's odduns. Although wracked with pain the babalawo completes the painstaking rituals that take well over an hour. He concludes the ceremony by taking the package to Echu, entrusting the oricha with the task of delivering the ebbó to Olodumare.

With the part of the ceremony employing the Table of Ifá completed the babalawo then sacrifices the rooster to Echu, letting the blood drip over the concrete face set in a conch shell, which contained and embodied the powerful Messenger of the Gods. The cowrie shell eyes seem to gleam as the oricha devours the offered blood. Finally, the scalpel is put to Ogún while asking the blacksmith oricha to ensure the surgeon's work is a success.

Ebbós are the sacrifices, offerings, and cleansings used in Ifá to help us rid ourselves of negativity, overcome obstacles, and help us attain more fulfilling lives. While many ebbós are not as complex as the one just described, all ebbós have one thing in common. They express the reciprocal nature of our relationships with the forces of nature and human endeavor. We share with them so that they may share with us. Ebbós are the system of efficient solutions built into Ifá divination, and like the one performed above, they are often specifically prescribed by the particular oddun that appears during an Ifá consultation. For many outside our tradition, the fact that some ebbós involve animal sacrifice makes it the most controversial and misunderstood facet of our tradition.

There are many different kinds of ebbós, and although each has its own purpose and meaning, Ifá prescribes almost all during an osode. An ebbó may be given to the egguns, or an oricha to enlist their aid, or they may be offered to appease forces that might otherwise harm us. The ebbó may also take the form of a *limpieza* (cleansing), or it could even be a complex ceremony designed to set into motion a series of events described in one of the odduns in Ifá. The ingredients of an ebbó can include fruits, plants, various objects, rituals, or animals depending on the nature of that particular oddun and the particular challenge facing the client. Through these acts we are able to avert disaster, improve our lives, and achieve balance with the forces around and within ourselves.

Reciprocity

Offerings and other ebbós should never be seen as a bribe to the egguns or orichas, but instead as part of a mutual relationship we learn to maintain with the powers that make up the world around us. The idea that we should have a direct relationship with nature based on a continual give-and-take is a fundamental principle of Ifá. In fact, reciprocity is the central principle behind many of Ifá's ebbós and is the basis of our daily dealings with egguns and the orichas as well—it is very simple really. We take care of the forces and beings of the world around us, and they take care of us. It is the same give-and-take that marks any relationship, whether it is with a friend, spouse, or the orichas and other Powers themselves. After all, what would you think of a person who constantly asked for things but never showed any real gratitude and did nothing for you? Even the most altruistic and giving person would quickly tire of such treatment and come to the conclusion that they are being used. It is no different with the dead or the orichas. With time this constant give-and-take helps us to build incredibly strong and lasting relationships with our egguns and the orichas. Remember that we don't *act* as if the orichas are real living beings. They *are* living beings. Anyone who has spent time in our tradition has no doubt of that because we have experienced far too many things to come to any other conclusion.

Ebbó as Resolution

In a world built up of numerous conflicting forces the ebbó is our foremost weapon for attaining or regaining balance. When a client comes to us in osogbo, or with something impeding their iré in their lives it is up to the babalawo, through the wisdom of Ifá, to come up with the proper ebbó to put that client's life in order. It should be mentioned that a person doesn't necessarily need to have done something wrong in order to be out of balance. We are in constant interaction with the forces and people around us, and therefore can come into contact with any number of things that can bring harm to us. A person may come into our lives bringing with them some form of negativity that can affect us. Someone may wish us harm out of envy, dislike, or even just because, or we may stumble on something through no fault of our own that could have an ill effect on us. There is any number of reasons why our lives might get thrown out of balance, and because balance is such a tenuous thing, we often need to act in order to regain balance in our lives.

Christians believe that the crucifixion was a sacrifice that cleansed the world of sin for all time. Of course for santeros such a sacrifice would be impossible because we see ourselves as being part of a world that is constantly changing to maintain a delicate balance. So for us there is no conceivable way to make a single ebbó that would cover all situations for all time. For all of us sacrifice is a necessary and desirable part of life, and just as we make sacrifices for the happiness and well-being of our human loved ones, we must also make the appropriate sacrifices to the forces around us to ensure our own well-being.

Types of Ebbós

As mentioned above, there are a number of different kinds of ebbós each serving different purposes and having different meanings. The most common ones are used for cleansing, strength, and protection. The most common types of ebbós can be found below.

Sarayeye

Also known as a limpieza, Sarayeye is one of the most common ceremonies performed to cleanse a person of negativity. In this ritual fruits, plants, animals, or sometimes cigar smoke or cologne are passed over the person's body to absorb any negativity on the person before they are offered to the dead or an oricha. The ingredients and what is done with them is prescribed by Ifá during the consultation to ensure the ceremony is as effective as possible because it is precisely what the orichas themselves ask for.

In most cases animals that have been sacrificed are cooked and eaten by everyone attending the ceremony so all may partake of the aché, but the sarayeye is an exception. The reason for this is that after the cleansing ceremony the bird has become saturated with the person's negativity, and anyone eating the bird would also be affected by that negativity. Therefore, in the case of a Sarayeye the animal's remains must be disposed of at a location the oricha or eggun chooses and never eaten.

Unfortunately, improper disposal of animal remains has brought our tradition a lot of negative and unwanted publicity. It is not uncommon in some areas to see a segment on the six o'clock news reporting that the carcass of an animal has been found in the middle of a public area, such as a park, and that it is likely to have been part of a Santería ritual. Of course the media often makes the situation worse than it really is by making additions like showing a photo of a kitten or puppy during the segment, while adding utterly inaccurate and negative descriptions of our religion. The fact that we don't sacrifice kittens and puppies doesn't seem to matter. The fact is that, besides small birds such as chickens, guinea hens, and pigeons, the only animals we sacrifice are goats, sheep, bush rats, and turtles.

To be fair, we must shoulder some of the blame for these incidents due to some practitioners' insensitivity to the feelings and rights of others. Too many times animal remains have been unceremoniously dumped where they can be found by some poor soul who will react in shock, disgust, and fear. This type of situation is easily avoided by taking a little extra care and time disposing the remains of the animal. For instance, if a bird must be taken to the *manigua* (the wilderness), it is usually not too difficult to find an area where people aren't likely to go, and put the remains in thick brush where it can't be easily found. And many times we can bury the animal, making it unlikely that some hapless mom with her children in tow will stumble upon it. Thus, a few extra steps can drastically reduce the number of incidents and negative publicity that follows such grisly discoveries. We need not be apologetic for our traditions, but neither should we flaunt them in the face of those who are least likely to understand them. This is an area where our customary secrecy, carried over from when we were even more actively persecuted, serves a very useful purpose.

Keborí Eledá or Rogación

The keborí eledá or rogación de la cabeza is a ceremony designed to cleanse, strengthen, refresh, and protect our Orí Eledá. Our orí is the destiny or path in life that we chose before coming to this world and is the most direct connection we have to the divine. Our orí also determines our luck and such resources as intelligence, our particular talents, strengths, and weaknesses.

Our heads are not just a home for our brains, but contain our destinies as well as being our most important resource. If our orí is in poor condition, it can affect every aspect of our lives and everything can go sour, including our luck and our health. A weakened or overheated head can also have a tendency to be confused and "off." On the other hand, a strong and refreshed head will have much more clarity, calm, and alignment. During a rogación certain ingredients are ritually applied to the head while the appropriate ceremonies are being performed. There are various types of rogación, some of which can only be performed by a babalawo. Even though the rogación is a relatively simple ceremony, it's importance and strength cannot be underestimated. This ceremony is performed as part of virtually every initiation as well, so your orí will be in accord with the ceremony and to achieve the maximum possible alignment during initiation.

Rompimiento

The rompimiento or breaking ceremony is used to forcibly separate a person from a negative force or being. It can be performed by a santera, a palero, or a babalawo. It is performed by breaking or tearing the clothes of the client before being given a cleansing with herbs or other materials and/or a cleansing bath. The rompimiento must be performed by a priestess or priest who is of the same gender as the client as it involves nudity.

Ebbó Misí (Baths)

Ebbó Misí are baths either prepared ceremonially using fresh herbs belonging to the orichas, or using ingredients such as flowers, *efún* (a type of white chalk commonly called by its Spanish name cascarilla), cologne, or any number of other ingredients. Many times the person is able to perform the prepared baths themselves at home. A priestess or priest, however, must perform some baths and in those cases the same rules apply as with the rompimiento to prevent any sort of impropriety from occurring.

Paraldo

The paraldo is the most effective ceremony performed to separate malevolent forces such as obsessive or negative spirits that may have become attached to a person or sent to attack them by another person. In fact, a paraldo could be best described as an extremely powerful type of exorcism. The paraldo is a ceremony that can only be performed by a trained babalawo because it involves the forces of multiple tremendously powerful odduns to tear the negative eggun from the person and entrap them. Once entrapped the exorcized spirit is dispatched where it can do no more harm to the person. This is an exceedingly sensitive ceremony and can be dangerous if done incorrectly.

Initiation

For some people it is their destiny to become a practitioner of our tradition and may require multiple initiations in order to achieve balance and alignment and to move forward. On occasion, a person will be called to be fully initiated in either the oricha and/or Ifá priesthood. Initiation into the priesthood is an extremely serious step because it is a life-changing event and should be considered a lifetime commitment. Initiation as a priest also requires a huge commitment from the initiate and can be considerably difficult. For instance, when a person is initiated as a santero, or oricha priest, they are expected to wear only white clothing, cannot touch other people, or take anything from their hands for an entire year. For three months they must eat while seated on a mat using only a spoon and cannot look into a mirror, in addition to other challenges. Full initiation as an oloricha or babalawo is definitely not something to be taken lightly.

Advice

Often during the course of an osode consultation Ifá will give advice to the client in addition to or in place of other offerings. This may include taboos such as foods, types of clothing, or places to be avoided or emphasized. For instance, Ifá may tell us to wear white clothes for a certain number of days, not to eat some certain foods such as pork or eggs, or to avoid going to certain places or doing specific activities. Sometimes though Ifá will ask us to make major changes in the way we act in general and toward other people. In my experience I've found that many clients have the most difficulty with this one. People are much more willing to go through the most elaborate and expensive cleansings and ceremonies than to put in the work necessary to change aspects of their personality that are causing problems and holding them back. And following advice usually doesn't cost the client a dime.

Ebbó de Tablero (Ebbó Katero)

The ebbó katero just may be the most powerful weapon in the babala-wo's arsenal. The ritual is extremely complex, sensitive, and time con-suming but it is one of the most powerful rites for cleansing and em-powering our clients. It involves the direct use of power of various odduns marked, prayed, and sung using the Table of Ifá during the course of that ebbó. The babalawo then breaks these odduns by rub-bing a packet containing the ingredients of the ebbó over the odduns marked on the table, infusing this packet with the power contained within these odduns. Each of these odduns serves a particular task in the ebbó. For example, the oddun Oché Tura sets the ebbó in motion, empowering it with the oddun's aché while the oddun Ocana Yekun is a gatekeeper who is called so the ebbó will be allowed to enter the world of orichas and eggun. All of these odduns are prayed and sung to honor and compel the forces around us to help the client who has come to us for aid, and to lend their forces to the ebbó and for whom the ebbó is performed. From there the client takes the ebbó and places it at the feet of Echu, who is in charge of delivering it to Olodumare. The ingredi-ents and animals of this ebbó are then distributed as designated through Ifá divination. The different items in the ebbó may be claimed by differ-ent orichas or may need to be taken to a special spot like a hill or wilder-ness area. For instance, oranges in an ebbó may need to go to Ochún, while Yemayá might claim a watermelon but it may need to be given to her at the ocean. Only babalawos can perform the ebbó katero because they are the only priesthood empowered to set the forces of the odduns in motion by marking them, reciting their prayers and songs, and per-forming the rituals associated with them. These abilities are bestowed on the babalawo by being initiated in the presence of Odun, who is the ultimate source for all the powers contained within the odduns.

As mentioned above, an ebbó performed on the Table of Ifá will of-ten contain ingredients used by a client in ancient times to resolve their situation in the stories that accompany an oddun. In this way the events of that oddun are replayed setting into motion the events described in that oddun.

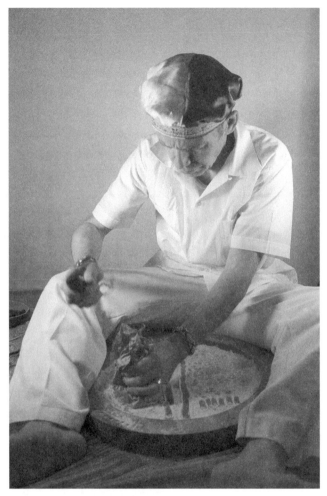

Babalawo performing Ebbó Katero

One day Olodumare decided he wanted to send children to the world, which up until this time was populated by only adults. The problem was the world was separated from heaven by a tremendous chasm. He called upon the orichas for their help in resolving this situation. One by one the orichas would grab some of the children and attempt to leap across the abyss with all their force, but in order to grab the edge on the other side, each oricha found they had to let go of the children, who

would then tragically fall to their deaths. Even the most powerful ori-
chas failed as they were inevitably forced to release the children to grip
the edge of the abyss, as the chasm was simply too wide for even the
most powerful oricha to land on their feet.

Finally, Olodumare went to Orunmila to see if he might be able to
resolve the problem. Orunmila told Olodumare that he would need five
days with which to see the situation and make the appropriate ebbó.
When Orunmila consulted for himself the oddun Ogbe Tumako came,
which called for an ebbó that included a rooster for Echu and a white
cloth. Orunmila made the ebbó. At the end of the five days Orunmila
went before Olodumare carrying the cloth and asked for two of the chil-
dren to carry across. When Olodumare handed over two of his chil-
dren, Orunmila used the white cloth to fashion a kind of sling or pa-
poose for himself and put the children on his back inside the folds of
cloth. This freed his hands so that he was able to grab the edge of the
world once he passed over the abyss. Thus, he was able to bring all of
Olodumare's children in ones and twos to this world. In appreciation
for having resolved the situation through wisdom instead of brute force,
Olodumare called on Orunmila to stand before him and show his
hands.

Olodumare then spat on each of his hands, giving Orunmila his
aché and with it the power to act as his second in command. "And from
this day forward, any oricha who wishes to do something must ask your
permission and will have to depend on you."

When a client who is having problems getting pregnant comes to
be seen with Ifá and the oddun Ogbe Tumako appears, the client will
likely be asked to make the same ebbó as Orunmila did, including the
white cloth. With these ingredients, the babalawo will then call that oddun into action, along with the use of the correct prayers and songs. In
this way the events described in the oddun can be re-enacted so that
they will play out in the life of the client and help to conceive. At this
point I should make it clear that this is not simply imitative magic
where ingredients symbolizing the desired result are used to accomplish the desired end. The patakís are stories with great power, and

through the use of these ebbós the events illustrated in the patakís are re-enacted as the oddun in question is marked and the prayers and songs used to greet and empower that oddun are performed.

Animal Sacrifice

Probably the single most misunderstood aspect of Santería pertains to animal sacrifice. Often those outside of the religion see the act of animal sacrifice as cruel, barbaric, and needless. The hypocrisy behind this becomes evident when you consider the fact that every time we eat a steak or enjoy a chicken sandwich living beings have been killed for that meal, and in the eyes of Olodumare life is life and the life of a plant is of equal importance as the life of an animal or human. The fact is, all of us feed on the death of others. There is no way of avoiding it. We must also keep in mind that one day each of us too will give up our lives for the benefit of other beings on this planet. In modern society the actual slaughter of these living beings is kept carefully hidden so we don't have to face the act of killing behind every meal we eat.

Sacrifice in some form is part of almost every religion in the world. Judaism has a ceremony known as kapparot performed just before Yom Kippur, the Jewish Day of Atonement, where a chicken is used to cleanse the practitioner before being slaughtered making it virtually identical to our Sarayeye rite. Even Christianity is based on sacrifice. In this case Jesus is the sacrifice who died to cleanse the world of sins. In Islam believers going on Haji or pilgrimage are directed to sacrifice a lamb or goat. And farther east Hindus perform animal sacrifice during the Yatral Jatra (festival) for Kandhen Budhi and during the Bali Jatra.

The orichas need the blood and the plants that make up the omiero in order to thrive and to aid us in our endeavors. These things are so crucial to our traditions that blood, stones, and herbs have been described as the core of our way of life. Animals slaughtered en masse by the meat industry are dispatched with much less care than we show the animals we sacrifice. The sheer number of songs, prayers, and rites that accompany every step of the animal sacrifice attest to the respect and regard given to the animals that are giving their lives so that ours may be bettered.

Remember the babalawo at the beginning of the chapter whose life was saved through performing the ebbó? That babalawo was me. I had gone to the doctor three times due to ongoing pain in my lower abdomen, where I was told to simply eat more fiber. I had pretty much given up on the doctors and was hoping that whatever was causing the pain would sort itself out over time. But one day when I saw myself with Ifá while on a trip to Northern California, an oddun appeared ordering me back to the doctor, as my life was at stake. This time I put a lot more pressure on the doctor to have me thoroughly checked out. Still unconvinced anything was seriously wrong with me, she prescribed some pain pills and ordered a CAT scan to "rule out anything crazy." That's when they found a grapefruit-sized tumor in my pelvic region.

A suitable specialist was found, surgery was quickly scheduled, and I consulted Ifá and found I needed to do the ebbó katero to ensure the operation would be a success. The surgery proved to be a long and difficult one. When I awoke from the anesthesia, the surgeon's first words to me were that I was a tough little guy and that I had lost forty percent of my blood during the surgery. I shouldn't have survived the surgery at all and will be eternally grateful to Orunmila, Obatalá, and Ogún—and to that little bird. I owe them my life.

Chapter Nine
Odduns

In a land called Nilé, when anyone died they had to go to a special priest called a Borokaton, who was more of a witch than a priest and was dedicated to trafficking with the dead and acting like a fortuneteller. The Borokaton used a tall clay pot that he claimed contained the secret of heaven within it.

When a person died, their family would take two hens and go to this Borokaton, who would then go to work. Before long they would hear the voice of the dead person coming from the jar. Also, any time a child was born they would use the jar to learn which spirit was the child's protector.

But there was a man named Gogo who went to the obá of this land, informing his liege of a man named Mokobí Awó who knew a system called Ifá, which he used to divine everything people needed to know about the past, present, and future. One year there came a huge drought, and it was a disaster. They went to every Borokaton in the land, but none of them knew how to make the rain come. Then the obá remembered what he had heard about this man named Mokobí Awó and called for him.

When Mokobí Awó arrived, he saw the obá with Ifá and marked the ebbó needed to make the rain fall anew and, in the process, prove Ifá was a True Seer.

Later the babalawo was called before the Royal Court to explain Ifá. Mokobí explained that Ifá consisted of sixteen Meyis or Olodus. And when Olodumare wanted to create something, he would use these sixteen Olodus, who each in turn had sixteen omolus, each of whom brought something different, and each Ifá was the owner of its own language.

He continued, telling them that all newborns had to be presented to a babalawo within the first three months of birth for divination to learn the child's destiny and which oricha they should worship.

Ifá knows the history of everything in the universe, both in this world and in Orun, the other world. He has command over the sacrifices that would make things right and to open the doors of the Other World to reveal the truth. And that each thing must be made happy first in Orun in order to be happy in this world thanks to Eleggúa and Ifá.

"The odduns of Ifá are stronger than any sorcery."

Ifá is a spiritual matrix containing everything in existence and every possible human experience. This matrix is made up of a grid composed of 256 odduns, cosmic archetypes representing the organization of aché in nature as well as the human situations that we may encounter in life. They are the living repositories containing the totality of the knowledge and information making up the world around us. And as we have seen, in Ifá the entire universe is regarded as being made up of knowledge and information and the world consists of information in conjunction with the consciousness apprehending that information. It is through knowledge, understanding, and consciousness of that information that change occurs in our universe. This is why Orula's role as Elerí Ikúín is such a profound one. Not only was he the sole witness to the original creation of the universe but he is also the indispensable witness as the universe is constantly created all around us. He is also the only oricha that knows the destinies of everything in the universe including the orichas and human beings.

One oddun in Ifá says children of a particular sign are connected to a special spirit which makes it possible for them to get anything they ask for, good or bad, by performing a simple ritual along with a prayer. But what the beginning babalawo doesn't know is when you translate the accompanying prayer for the ritual, it is simply asking the spirit to "enlighten me"!

Ifá's joke here reminds me of a story from Ch'an (Zen) Buddhism about Chao-chou's famous stone bridge. It was said that the bridge would impart enlightenment to anyone who crossed it. Monks would go on pilgrimages to see the bridge, sometimes traveling hundreds of miles on foot. When they finally arrived, however, they found the famous stone bridge was merely a bunch of logs over a stream, but just as with Ifá's trick, upon seeing this "famous stone bridge" some would indeed attain sudden enlightenment.

But the real punch line lies in the fact that knowledge or information apprehended in the right way really can make anything happen, good or bad. The babalawo is given another clue in a refrán from the same oddun. "Wisdom, understanding, and thought are the forces that move the world." This is the ultimate secret of the universe.

What Is an Oddun?

Named after their mother Odun, the word itself can be translated to chief or head, it also implies something big and bulky. They make up the core of Ifá. Everything in existence comes into being in these odduns and in them you can find the histories of each of the orichas as well as all of our religion's customs, ceremonies, and rituals. In fact, our entire oral tradition can be found within the odduns of Ifá. Therefore, the babalawo is trained not only to be a diviner and a healer but also to be the caretaker of our oral traditions. Orunmila and Odun gave birth to the original odduns, which are organized into sixteen *Olodduns* (kings of the odduns or meyis) that consist of the same pattern on each side. These sixteen eventually gave birth to the *omolus* (children of the kings, or combination odduns), which make up the remainder of the 256 odduns.

Although the omolus often share characteristics of their parent odduns they are considered individuals, and are much more than merely the combination of the meyis that gave birth to them. This is one of the characteristics of Ifá that separate it from the traditional diloggún divination used by iworos to divine the will of the orichas.[1]

+

I I

0 0

0 0

0 0

A Meyi (in this case Obara Meyi)

+

0 I

I I

0 I

I 0

An Omoluo (Ogundá Fun)

These odduns are like a huge database containing a massive amount of information or knowledge within them. Each oddun has its own plants, ceremonies, ritual recipes, offerings, things born in the particular oddun, patakís, refránes, and advice called *dice Ifá* (Ifá says) to orient and guide the person being seen by the babalawo. Each oddun even has its own path of Echu containing secrets and keys to working with the oddun to be shared only among babalawos. Odduns also have their own orikis and *suyeres* (chants) that accompany them. One class of orikis, called llamadas, are used to call the odduns and set them into action. These llamadas are ultimately the keys to unlocking the powers of everything in the universe. They are often short in length because their only purpose is to set the oddun into action. Others are longer and more involved because they are the specific incantations used to bring about a specific effect. The power that makes these llamadas work comes from the goddess Odun who is the ultimate source of the odduns and who rules over them. This is why she must be present during the initiation of every babalawo and why those who have received her are considered the highest rank within the babalawo hierarchy.

Every oddun contains a myriad of ancient parables called patakís graphically illustrating how that oddun works in your life, how you got there and where that path is headed. The use of stories to describe the how each of the odduns works in day-to-day life is genius itself.

Odduns also include refránes, which are proverbs describing the nature of the oddun condensed into one or two sentences. The patakís and refránes are poetic, profound, and multi-layered like an onion— you gain deeper insights as you peel off each layer. As mentioned in the introduction there is hardly a day that goes by that I don't re-visit a refrán or pataki and find new depth and meaning to it that I never saw before. I live for these moments of *eureka*! Although only a babalawo is consecrated to interpret the patakís and refránes, you don't have to be a babalawo to learn from them.

The Birth of the Pataki

The pataki is a Lucumí adaptation of the Yoruba ese Ifá, which are essentially the same parables in the form of verses or poems, a brilliant mnemonic device allowing the student to learn the parables much quicker and easier. In fact, Western medical students often learn anatomy using similar methods. In practice Yoruba babalawos recite the ese Ifá verses for the client's oddun until the client hears one that applies to the situation that led them to come to Ifá and this stops the babalawo's recitation.

These verses not only contained the stories and possible ebbós associated with the oddun. They often contained proverbs usually in the form of the names of mythical babalawos who consulted Ifá in the poem. For example, the babalawos' names in one of the patakís in chapter 6 were If You Teach Someone to Be Intelligent, They Will Become Truly Intelligent and If You Teach Someone To Be Stupid, They Will Become Truly Stupid. This was a clever means of imbedding the proverbs into the verse itself.

To practice Ifá in the traditional Yoruba way you must be completely fluent in the Yoruba language, which makes it difficult for a non-Yoruba to learn, and in Cuba few people spoke Yoruba fluently. Then there was the issue of different dialects that might be spoken by the few people who were still Yoruba speakers. Therefore the ese Ifá, as useful as it had been in Yorubaland, became impractical on the island. So the early babalawos expanded on the Yoruba Eyo Ifá to transform the ese verses into stories, calling them patakís or important things. The word pataki reveals the thinking of the old babalawos because the stories, proverbs, and depth of advice they give are indeed the important things within the ese Ifá. Thus, the early babalawos were able to construct an equivalent to the ese Ifá that could be used successfully in Cuba.

Spiritual Database

The odduns put together form an immense spiritual database. Along with the advice given by an oddun there are a myriad of sacrifices and offerings or cleansings called ebbós intrinsic to that oddun. These ebbós allow the babalawo to provide a solution that is particularly suited to that oddun and its path. While some of these ebbós can be used for more than one oddun many are specific to only that Ifá sign and could be ineffective if a person does not have that sign come up during divination. Some odduns require the babalawo perform a ritual whenever it appears during a consultation. For instance, when a certain oddun shows up the babalawo would immediately put *epó* (palm oil) to the mouth of everyone in the room. There are also various iches and recipes that help achieve certain results spoken about in the oddun, such as winning a court case, healing a disease, or achieving financial success. Sometimes though a person will be told not to chase after money as their hunger for wealth will destroy them. In fact, in Ifá money is considered cursed by its very nature and when we see the destruction caused by the corrupting effects money has had in the world we see the wisdom of Ifá.

In January 2008, hundreds of babalawos gathered in Havana for the Letter of the Year ceremony to learn what the new year would bring. A pataki from the oddun of that year, Iwori Rote, spoke of a young man surrounded by businessmen who fawned over him due to his money and possessions. They turned from being brown-nosing sycophants into his worst enemies overnight, leaving him without a home or his life savings. Of course this is exactly what happened to thousands, perhaps millions of people that year and the world economy was very nearly destroyed in the process.

Each oddun also has numerous plants associated with it, and their powers are invoked through prayers and songs from their respective odduns when we use the plants. For example, we sing *"Osain ewe bana oyu awa, ewe bana o forire"* to unlock the powers of the *ewe bana* (soapberry) plant that comes from the oddun Ogbe Sa. This song can be translated to "Osain, soapberry plant which is under your watchful eye, O soapberry plant bring us your blessings." Osain is the oricha of the herbs and the wilderness.

Most of our customs and rituals are re-enactments from our ancient past and originate in our odduns. Our entire oral tradition is recorded in the odduns so they also serve as divine precedents. Disagreements are often resolved by drawing on the wisdom coming from them and sometimes you will see one elder challenge another by demanding what oddun a ritual or custom originated. A younger priest must be very careful about questioning an elder in this manner, however, because most often they will not be answered for the young priest will be considered too big for their britches and unworthy of being taught. In our religion knowledge is slowly accumulated over many years and is much too precious to be given away simply because a young and inexperienced priest demands it. "The ears do not pass over the head" is the proverb most often used by elders to tell young priests that they need to learn at the pace and in the manner set by their elders.

Our mythic histories, like those of many indigenous peoples, are very different from Western histories because they serve very different purposes. The early Lucumís are likely to have found the history favored by Western historians and many ethnologists with their obsession with statistics and often meaningless details to be uninteresting and serving little purpose. Instead, our histories are meant to ensure the survival of our culture, knowledge, ethics, and worldview. We tell our history and perform the rituals from our past to continue our culture and knowledge in the present to ensure them for the future.

Every oddun has long lists of the things born and ruled over by it. These include anything found in nature and every possible human experience. The information and advice in an oddun can be extremely detailed, even down to what foods you should or should not eat. Each oddun has its own nature and personality that is inherited by everything and everyone, human or oricha, born under the auspices of that oddun. By knowing and using the right keys to unlock the power of that oddun a babalawo can affect any of the things ruled by the oddun.

Just like people each oricha came to this world accompanied by an oddun. This oddun is called their oddun isalayé, and their life stories can be found within this oddun isalayé and other odduns. Sometimes when a babalawo is faced with having to make a sacrifice to one of the orichas and doesn't have that oricha on hand, there is a ceremony where the babalawo can use the oddun combined with certain prayers and rituals to make the sacrifice. Of course, besides an oricha's oddun isalayé, there are a number of odduns where the oricha speaks and the oricha figures prominently.

As each oddun is a living being and a power unto itself each oddun has one or more paths of Echu associated with it to act as its messenger and empower it. People often find it is necessary to receive an Echu belonging to their oddun in kofá or abo faca. Each of these paths of Echu is made differently, some having twenty or more ingredients besides the standard ingredients that can be found in all Echus. Even modern inventions and events such as nuclear bombs, space travel, and biological warfare can be found in the patakís accompanying the odduns. In one pataki scabs taken from smallpox victims were used by priests of Babalú Ayé, the oricha of diseases, to infect enemy nations with the dreaded disease. This history illustrates a detailed understanding how diseases were spread that predates Pasteur by hundreds, if not thousands, of years not to mention the actual concept of biological warfare.

Odduns in Practice

Every oddun has specific powers that can be drawn upon to resolve any situation we might be faced with, and babalawos always eager to expand their arsenals spend lifetimes collecting secret recipes and incantations associated with them. I am constantly amazed at what a simple *afoché* (powder) made by marking the right odduns on the Table of Ifá can accomplish.

When I was a relatively new babalawo I had a young mother come to me in desperation. She and her only son were facing a court case and were looking at deportation. I knew we had a monumental task in front of us and frankly I held out little hope as I had seen immigration courts in action and seen judges summarily deporting everyone who came before them. But Ifá assured us that everything would be resolved by making an afoché powder using the Table of Ifá, which she was to blow onto the four corners of the courthouse before the hearing took place. When I didn't hear a word from her for months I assumed they had been deported. As I was such a new babalawo perhaps I had left an important step out, but about four months later I got a call from her asking for help with another issue. Of course I asked about what had happened at the deportation.

"Oh, that," she said as if it were nothing. "The judge said we could stay in the country. Now about this new problem..."

Such is the life of a babalawo.

During the ceremony known as the Ebbó Katero sometimes as many as forty or more odduns are used, making it one of the most potent weapons in the babalawo's arsenal. Every time I go to Havana Padrino Miguelito gives me more odduns to add to my ebbó making it longer and longer. But when he tells me what the new odduns are used for and how they will make my ebbó more powerful I go about memorizing the new prayers. And sometimes all you need is the correct prayers from an oddun or two to solve your problems.

One day Padrino Miguelito and I were making the long drive through the Cuban countryside on our way to a ceremony in the midst of a huge storm. By the time we reached the halfway point, the storm had become so powerful that we were endangered by it, with water pouring down in buckets and lightning striking all around us. Padrino Miguelito began to recite special prayers from two odduns that had the power to stop the rain and wind. Within minutes not only had the storm subsided but the sun was shining as if the downpour had never existed. As luck would have it, less than a week later I would have the need to use those newly learned prayers myself when a severe rain threatened to ground all the planes at the airport. Again, within minutes the downpour subsided and the sun reappeared to take the place of the tempest.

Everything in existence originates in the odduns, and with enough knowledge of them anything can be accomplished.

Chapter Ten

Ways of Power:
Aché atí Ogbogba—Power and Balance

One day Orula was seeing himself with Ifá and learned that Ikú was on her way to Orula's house to take him away. The wise oricha was therefore well prepared, and when Ikú arrived at Orula's house he had covered the floor of his house with a slimy paste of quimbombó (okra), and was waiting for her along with Elegguá, Ogún, and Changó. When Death entered Orula's house she immediately slipped on the slimy ooze on the floor. As Death was falling Elegguá seized her scythe and Ogún instantly tangled her up in chains.

Changó yelled, "Do you not see that this is Orunmila? And now you will pay for your evil designs!" And with a mighty roar Changó unleashed a huge ball of flames from his mouth, burning Ikú severely. Changó then raised his axe and was just about to bring it down on Death's neck when Orula entered the room.

"Wait," shouted Orula, and Changó stopped his ax mere inches from Ikú's head.

"I am not going to finish you off today, Ikú," said Orula. "I will save your life but we must make a binding pact, here and now. I realize it is your task to bring an end to everyone's life and I know it is a necessary one," Orula continued. "But from now on you cannot take me or any of my children without my permission."

"Very well," agreed Ikú, who had little choice but to accept Orula's offer, *"but how will I know your children?"*

"You will know my children by the iddé of green and yellow beads that they shall wear, and from this day forward you shall never take any of my children without my permission. To iban Echu."

"The world is broken. Orula will mend it."

Aché and balance are the two interlocking concepts underlying Ifá's exceptional effectiveness and power and are crucial to fully understanding Ifá. Virtually everything we do in Ifá is aimed at achieving, maintaining, or restoring balance with the powers within and around us. These principles form the basis of Ifá philosophy and our worldview informing everything from our ceremonies to our ethics and morality.

Aché: Power

We live in a world of power—a living power that permeates everything that exists. Originating at the moment of creation, it pervades everything in the universe. This power is called aché and every force or object has its own particular type of aché that can be used to almost any end imaginable.

Everything we see around us is made of aché and without it nothing would occur. In fact, aché is sometimes defined as the power to make things happen. Pure aché is raw, undifferentiated power and knows no good or evil. It simply *is*, and from that pure aché, all that we consider good or bad is manifested. Any kind of effectiveness, luck, talent, or success comes from a person's personal aché.

How do we access this power? Well, there are a number of ways. We can access this power through rituals and offerings to the egguns, the orichas, and our own orís. Then there are initiations where we actually receive powers or even have orichas melded with us during the initiations as oricha priests and as babalawos. We can attain power through certain types of dreams and babalawos can access and acquire power directly through Ifá's odduns themselves.

The odduns are the cosmic archetypes of aché. Representing all the different ways that aché can manifest the odduns form a grid or matrix of aché in all its forms with each oddun having its own personality and function. The odduns rule over everything in the universe and each have special powers, prayers, songs, rituals, and secrets to activate them. And it is knowledge of the odduns that allow the babalawo to acquire such immense power. Knowledge or information is what underlies every force and every element in the universe. Therefore, for the Lucumí babalawo knowledge *is* power.

Sometimes aché is defined as authority or command because it is seen as the source of all command and authority among the Lucumís and the Yoruba. Although an obá is usually born into that position rituals are performed on them to confer the aché necessary to rule. In the religion, each person is infused with aché during their initiation, which gives them the authority and ability to practice as an oloricha or babalawo. This authority is not only licencia. It is also to be infused with the aché that gives us the power to work in these roles.

Aché in its more powerful forms can be extremely dangerous if not approached correctly, and there are rituals during the major initiation ceremonies that are designed to ensure the neophyte is strong enough to be able to withstand the tremendous power of the aché they are infused with during their initiation. In the case of the olorichas the actual power of the orichas are aligned and fused with their orí, and in the case of a babalawo Orunmila's aché is fused with their being.

Aché is something we are born with but can also be acquired. We are born with the aché that defines our personalities and talents, as well as our luck and success, but it must be cultivated or it can be lost. If that occurs rituals must be performed to help restore that aché. On the other hand, living our lives and our destinies well will help us accumulate aché. It can also be acquired through rituals to the egguns, orichas, other forces and sometimes through certain kinds of dreams.

All forms of aché originate in Orun and are reflected in our world. Orun is ancient, primordial, and outside of historic time and space yet is present here and now. Echu is the gatekeeper between these worlds, making him indispensable to Orula and to the babalawo. The crossroads between the worlds is represented on the opon Ifá or Table of Ifá, one of the principal tools enabling the babalawo to create openings to access this aché. Even we originate in the other world, which is why we say "The world is a marketplace, the other world is our true home." Although we spend our earthly existence here in the world we must never forget where we come from and where we will eventually return. The more we live in alignment with this other world the better and more fruitful our lives will be.

As we discussed earlier, Olodumare and Olófin largely retired from many of the day-to-day functions of running the universe and divided these duties among their intermediaries, the orichas. So instead of going to Olodumare or Olófin for our needs we go to the oricha who rules over the area of life that we are seeking guidance in.

This raw power becomes less diffused and becomes more defined as it is divided up into the different types of aché under the domain of the various orichas. For instance, we might go to Ochún who embodies the aché ruling over matters of the heart for help in our love lives, or we might go to the warriors orichas Oggún or Changó to defend ourselves.

Similarly, each of us is born with certain types of aché. Our aché comes from the oddun we are born with, and we also share the aché that our master oricha embodies. For example, if you are a child of Changó, you are likely to be a very persuasive talker and apt to have an ability to learn things more quickly than others around you. These gifts would be considered part of your aché. If you are generally lucky and good things seem to fall into your lap it is a likely sign you are presently in a state of iré and in tune with the powers in and around you, particularly your orí.

Sometimes it is revealed that a person requires a short ceremony called a keborí eledá or rogación de la cabeza. This ritual, whose ingredients range from the very simple to the very complex, is designed to propitiate, strengthen, and cleanse your orí. The effects of this brief ceremony are felt immediately. One feels calm, refreshed, and airy. I have even had people feel so euphoric afterward that they need their spouse to drive them home. The effects can be far-reaching, with improved luck, clarity, and tranquility. Even one's general success and health have been affected after the ritual has been performed. Every aspect of your life can be improved with this relatively simple ceremony. It is not surprising that there are many types of keborí eledás depending on the person's needs and the wishes of their orí. These range from the simplest rogación to a keborí eledá with specialized ingredients and extra ceremonies that align the person's head directly with Olófin, and which can only be performed by babalawos. This ritual is pivotal and is performed before virtually every initiation. Deceptively simple and short, it just may be the most important type of ebbó available and should be performed regularly to keep oneself properly aligned.

Again, for the Lucumí babalawo, knowledge is power and power is life. As we saw in chapter 1 knowledge is what underlies every force and every element in the universe. This power is not only alive but is what imparts life to every living being. In Ifá, power and the ability to live in balance is achieved primarily through gaining knowledge. It is the possession of knowledge that helps us to access this aché by putting us in closer contact with the forces underlying all of nature and learning to work with those forces. Knowledge is acquired through learning and understanding the rituals, patakís, refránes, and songs. The ceremonies we perform and experience imbues us with that knowledge as well. And finally, our experiences in life, both good and bad, show us how these forces unfold and help us to gain a deeper understanding of how they work.

Balance

A young woman travels down a thin path bordered by a white line on one side and a black line on the other. Cautioned to stay within the lines, she carefully winds her way through the darkness toward her encounter with only small candles on the floor to help find her way.

The Lucumí worldview is tremendously sophisticated, embracing paradoxes and opposites as part of a complex and constantly changing balance rather than the rigid and simplistic dualistic view of the world found in most Western European thought. In Ifá we see the universe as well as ourselves as being in a constant struggle to achieve, maintain, or restore balance. This is because we are surrounded by a multitude of forces perpetually confronting and interacting with one another each with their own trajectories and aims, and each in a constant state of flux and change.

In the Western worldview where the universe is viewed as a battle-ground between good and evil we quickly run into insurmountable paradoxes. For instance, what if a person had killed Hitler at an early age? Wouldn't that make that person a murderer even if it had saved millions of Jews, Gypsies, gays, and dissidents? The Western view of the world also places us separate from, and at odds with, the world around us. This view also often goes as far as to separate us from our own bodies, which are considered to be base and corrupt by nature. In Ifá that is considered to be an overly simplistic and ultimately untenable view of the world.

Another way of looking at Ifá's view of balance is to think of our-selves as spending our lives walking down that path bordered by a white line on one side and black line on the other, or, between the two legs of the oddun we were born under. If we stray too far to one side or the other we will find ourselves out of bounds or out of balance and fac-ing serious problems. In other words we too are constantly attempting to maintain balance between black and white, good and evil, life and death. Instead of viewing the world as an eternal war between good and evil the Lucumí lives in a holistic world where bad can be good and good can be bad. Our patakís are filled with examples illustrating just how bad acts can, and often do, lead to a good end and good acts can ultimately lead to an unfortunate finish.

The more something or someone is thrown out of balance the more catastrophic it will be for that balance to be restored. The present global warming crisis is a good example of a major imbalance in the world, as well as alternatives to how that balance can be restored. The unre-strained use of fossil fuels combined with deforestation has caused a massive imbalance on our planet. If mankind is unable to restore that balance through changes in our behavior nature will intervene and achieve balance in a much more catastrophic way. This could happen with devastating rises in sea levels, extreme weather, expansions of deserts, the mass extinction of species, or even trigger a new Ice Age. Balance will be achieved one way or another, even if humans become extinct in the process.

One of a babalawo's first acts in virtually any ritual is to salute the dead, the orichas, and Ifá with a long prayer known as the moyuba. As part of this moyuba it is customary to include "Iba irunmole yikotún, iba awamole yikosí." This prayer salutes the 400 powers to our right and the 200 powers to the left. These numbers aren't meant to be taken literally; they acknowledge the vast number of powers or forces that surround us. These forces include things such as the orichas and other forces that from our point of view we consider good, such as the irés of health, gains, and intelligence as well as forces we often consider bad such as death, disease, or loss. It is far too simplistic for us to take a dualistic approach to the world and to consider these forces to be merely good or bad. For instance, most of us would consider death to be a bad thing, especially when we face the death of someone dear to us, but in the big picture death is a very necessary thing. If there were no death life would be unsustainable. If plants, animals, and people didn't die there would be nothing to fertilize the soil. Without fertile soil plants can't grow, leaving animals, including humans, without anything to eat or the ability to create new life—not to mention the problems that would come from severe overpopulation. Also, if we lived forever we would never feel the urgency or need to accomplish anything in our lives. Without death life would be truly miserable and ultimately not worth living.

We do not attempt to subject the world to our will. Instead we align ourselves with the powers that surround us. Especially with our own orí and being that we are able to lead a more fulfilling life and to overcome the obstacles that life presents to us. In this spirit Ifá often deals with the malign or evil forces through mollification rather than attempting to openly combat them. "Skill is of more value than force."

So there must always be balance between the forces of the universe or everything would be in a state of abject chaos. If we look around us we see it is so, even on a cosmic level, as without this balance of forces there would be nothing preventing the earth from flying headlong into the sun, or the universe from flying apart. It is Orunmila's job, with the aid of the much-maligned Echu, to achieve and maintain balance between these forces. We sometimes speak of Echu as being the 401st Irunmole on the right as well as being the ruler of all the Ajogun or Irunmole to the left. Thus, he is allied with eggun, the orichas, and all the irés, and at the same time with the forces that bring the calamities in life. And so it must be. It is Echu's unique role in the universe that makes him Orunmila's closest friend and most valued helper. This privileged relationship between Echu and Orunmila is one of the things that make Ifá so powerful.

In the oddun Ogbe Funfun Nlo it is said that the world is broken and that Ifá will mend it. In reality, the world is constantly being thrown out of balance and Orula is constantly fixing it. Balance is a precarious thing, or as the martial artist Bruce Lee once put it "Balance is running like hell to keep it." The fact is that the world is continuously out of balance and has new balances being achieved to accommodate those changes. Thus, a certain amount of imbalance is necessary for growth and change but ultimately balance must be restored, but is temporary. The only constants are change, balance lost, and balance regained, only to be lost and regained again. The need for imbalance for the world to advance is illustrated in the following patakí, which shows that even war can be a necessary thing.

> When Olófin assigned the different types of aché to the orichas Obatalá Ayáguna was chosen to be a warrior and the creator of revolutions, and wherever Ayáguna went he ruled by force of arms and spread revolution over much of Africa.
>
> One day Olófin sent for Ayáguna and asked him, "Why do you start so many revolutions if my wish is to have peace for all?"
>
> To this Ayáguna responded, "With all due respect, you are always seated upon your throne, far away from it all, and your blood does not coarse through your veins in the same way as ours."
>
> The ceaseless combat continued between Ayáguna and his neighbors and Olófin was constantly trying to reign in Ayáguna's warlike behavior. Finally, Olófin decided to see if his quarrelsome nature would

be tempered by a change of location so Olófin sent the warrior Obatalá to Asia, and it is said that during this time Ayáguna was also given the task of teaching Ifá to the Chinese.

When Ayáguna arrived in China he found the people were far too passive and peace loving. When he tried to teach them Ifá he found they were only interested in telling the future and refused to follow Ifá. Ayáguna thought to himself, "They will have to learn to fight for their own good, or they will forever be ruled by tyrants." He also decided to only teach them a lite version of Ifá with only six parts to their signs instead of eight.

Intent on teaching them a lesson the warrior Obatalá went to a neighboring country and instilled the idea that the Chinese were passive and therefore ripe for conquest. Then he returned to China where he rallied the people there and informed them that their neighbors were coming to invade them and that they were now forced to fight. Thus, he went about traveling the world, fanning the flames of discord and war among humanity.

Finally, some people went to Olófin to complain that Ayáguna was constantly provoking wars. Olófin then went to the warrior Obatalá saying, "Please, my son. I wish peace. I am peace. I am Ala Morere, the White Flag of Peace."

To this Obatalá Ayáguna replied, "Without discord in the world, there is no progress. Without revolt, and the threat of revolt, there is only tyranny and peace and harmony through tyranny is a fraud. Yes, it is messy, but that is how the world moves forward."

Olófin, seeing the truth in Ayáguna's words, said with a deep sigh, "Very well. Thus the world will continue until the day you turn your back on wars and decide to lay down to rest."

That day has not yet come …

Imbalance is as necessary as balance, and as this pataki reveals, imbalance is necessary for there to be forward motion in the world and for us to advance and grow as people. Without imbalance life quickly becomes static and stale, and the imbalances that occur in our lives are usually what propel us to excel as we change and acquire a new balance. In much the same way everything in the world requires imbalance in order to grow and change. This invaluable concept is also reflected in the proverb at the beginning of the chapter with its implication that the world is perpetually broken, just as Orula is perpetually mending the world. As odd and contradictory as it may seem, imbalance is actually an important part of balance.

On a personal level, when our virtues and strengths become unbalanced, they become our vices and weaknesses. For example, spontaneity is a great virtue. It enlivens us and those who around us, and enables us to successfully confront unexpected situations and to think well on our feet. However, when spontaneity is thrown out of balance it becomes impulsiveness, and we become flighty and unstable. In the extreme we can become dangerously erratic. On the other hand, to be reliable and steadfast can also be a virtue. The ability to persevere allows us to succeed against all odds where others fail, and it provides security and protection for those around you. When out of balance that steadfastness becomes an inability to be flexible resulting in serious problems, particularly in relationships. Not only may the person become tedious to those around them, they can find themselves unable to deal with any unexpected event, even a dangerous one. Therefore, it becomes crucial to constantly seek balance within ourselves and with the forces that surround us. Sometimes we are thrown out of balance by our own actions or inaction and sometimes we are thrown out of balance through the intervention of other forces or people.

The central means of achieving, maintaining, and restoring balance to our lives is ebbó. Often it is much more than a simple offering of candles, fruits, or animals and may involve complex and sophisticated rituals, such as the ebbó katero, or an initiation to put us in alignment with one or more orichas.

In Ifá rather than make a futile attempt to fight the forces that are harmful and more powerful than us, we may instead seek to appease and assuage them. For example, if ikú wants to take us in order to feed the earth we might offer to give the earth something else such as a chicken or goat to hold things off for the time being. Thus, through Ifá a deal is brokered and balance is achieved in a way that is not catastrophic to ourselves or those that are dear to us.

There may be no better way to illustrate our view of balance than to explore one of the most important, and unfortunately most misunderstood concepts in Ifá. Iwá Pele.

Iwá Pele and Mo Iwá Fun Oniwá

Usually translated as good character or gentle character, the concept of iwá pele has not only become overused, but also grossly oversimplified, especially when thought of in the Western European sense of the word character. How does this good character match up with the fact that we are all born in one of the 256 odduns in Ifá where there is a vast variety of personality types or types of character to be found within these signs? Does the idea of iwá pele really denote a cookie-cutter idea of an ideal of good character, or is true iwá pele a much more variable and fluid concept? And just how fluid and variable is that concept?

First of all, the mere definitions of the words iwá and pele show a far greater depth and complexity than the Western words "good character" offer us, and show a profound understanding of the human condition not often seen in the Western world. The term iwá has been translated alternatively as character, existence, and destiny in dictionaries, and the famous Yoruba author Wole Soyinka defines iwá as personality. These definitions reveal an important aspect of our worldview where character, existence, and destiny are not separate and different ideas. Instead they are parts of a greater whole. For us the destiny we are born with not only defines our character, but paints an accurate picture of what our existence will look like as well. Therefore character, existence, and destiny are inseparable from our point of view.

Next, the word pele is variously translated as calm, gentle, cautious, and serious, which when taken together suggest a general state of calm thoughtfulness and balance. Therefore, a more accurate definition of iwá pele could be character brought into balance through the careful and thoughtful application of a thorough knowledge of our destiny.

Needless to say, this definition is a far cry from the vague, yet rigid, idealized behavior we would associate with the words good character in the Western sense. Like most idealized behavior, the problem is that no one could possibly live up to such a definition of good character. What isn't so well-known is that the term iwá pele is often accompanied by a traditional Yoruba phrase that isn't mentioned in many of the books or discussions on iwá pele. *"Mo iwá fun oniwá"* translates to "acknowledge each person's own individual character." This gives us a different view than offered by the oversimplified and westernized idea of good character.

The idea is that a person's ideal character or existence can vary widely depending on the oddun that defines each individual destiny. Furthermore, what is correct behavior for a person born in one oddun can be detrimental or even disastrous to a person born in another oddun, as each of us are born with different assets, strengths, talents, and weaknesses as well. To illustrate the true nature of the concept of Mo iwá fun oniwá, here is a pataki entitled *Those Who Imitate, Fail*:

> *There was a farmer who had a beautiful and beloved horse who refused to be dominated or controlled by anyone. No matter how much the farmer tried this horse just simply could not be tamed. Over time the horse's owner finally realized he could never control the beautiful beast, and not having the heart to kill or sell it, he decided to set it free.*
>
> *The ox, seeing how the horse had won its liberty through his acts of rebellion cleverly decided to employ the same tactic to win his freedom. The ox became fiercely rebellious, refusing to work and breaking through his pen every chance he got. At first the ploy worked as the ox's owner kept feeding and taking care of him. But as time went on the ox got fatter and fatter until finally one day the owner gave up on the ox much as he had done with the horse. But instead of setting the ox free the farmer simply sold the rebellious ox to a local butcher for meat.*

Here we have two individuals performing the same actions with two completely different consequences. Through identical acts of rebellion one animal gained its freedom while the other became dinner.

Not being true to your own destiny and existence could not only end in failure, but can even lead to disaster. One person's meat can be another person's poison.

None of this should be taken as license to act badly and simply blame it on your oddun. This is what is referred to as living your osog-bos that will inevitably lead to personal disaster and to a long list of serious consequences warned about in each oddun. Again, balance is the key here. To live your true nature and personality in a balanced way is being yourself and is a fundamental part of being in balance with the world. Otherwise you live your life undoing yourself, and you will find what you make with your hands you are destroying with your feet.

Chapter Eleven
Women and Feminine Power in Ifá

When Olófin created the world, the sixteen Meyis and Oché Turá were sent down to earth to put the world in order. As they all prepared to leave, they were told that although Oché Turá was below the Mejis, they must rely on her help in everything they did and declared her to be the Owner of Aché.

When the Mejis arrived on earth, they simply didn't see why they needed to count on her help. After all, she wasn't a Meji, and she was just a woman.

But the Mejis soon found that everything they attempted ended in failure. Nothing worked. Rain did not fall, plants did not grow, animals only lived for a short time before dying, and illness and famine covered the world. In short, all their great plans came to nothing, and everything they attempted was quickly spoiled.

But that was not the worst of it. Upon learning of the Mejis arrogance and lack of respect, Olófin sent Changó down to punish the sixteen Mejis' while they were holding a meeting. Changó hurled a huge lightning bolt down, burning the sign Oché Turá into the Table of Ifá and setting fire to the house.

Suddenly Olófin appeared and decreed, "From this day forward, every babalawo must write Oché Tura on the right and at the top of the Table of Ifá every time they perform ebbó. To iban Echu."

From that day on, we mark Oché Turá first whenever we make any kind of ebbó on the Table of Ifá—otherwise the ebbó will not be effective.

"Before a king can become sacred, a woman must give birth to him."

The role of women and feminine power is crucial to Ifá. Odun/Olófin, the manifestation of the Supreme Being from whose womb all creation sprang forth, is the highest power that can be received in Ifá and is the true source of Ifá's power. Without her presence there cannot be an initiation of an Ifá priest, and without the intervention of the apetebí there can be no Ifá initiation. Without women and feminine power there is no Ifá and no babalawos.

Virtually everything in Ifá and Santería revolves around a balance of shared power between the male and female. At the very top the manifestations of the Supreme Being Olodumare and Odun/Olófin are conceived as two parts of a closed calabash, containing this universe and all the others, where the two aspects of the Supreme Being become one. Odun/Olófin is the source of all creation and power in our universe and is the manifestation that is most accessible to us human beings as she took an interest in our particular universe while Olodumare went on to create other universes. As we said before, all powers and matter of the universe are contained in Odun/Olófin, sometimes known as Igba Odun Iwá or Odun, the Calabash of All Existence. Everything we see around us was born in one or another of her children, the odduns, which she gave birth to and is named after her. In turn half of the odduns are considered females with the other half being males, and each oddun also has a female and male side.

The concept of a closed calabash with two halves touches upon almost everything in our tradition. Ifá and Ocha are considered two parts of the calabash of one single religion, each with a different role and with both parts depending on one another. Within both Ifá and Ocha you see both male and female aspects. In the Lucumí religion, women have traditionally played a powerful role, and almost every rama of the religion has a woman as its root. The balance of power between women and men is reflected in the cabildos where La Regla Ocha was formed. The vast majority of the cabildos were jointly headed by a babalawo and a powerful santera. Of all the cabildos, the Cabildo Africano Lucumí was probably the most influential of all and is considered to have been the epicenter of

Lucumí culture. It was headed by the seminal babalawo Adechina along with the female cofounder Ña Caridad Argudín (Aigoró), who was likely to have been the ultimate root of the largest branch of the religion, the Pimienta. Within the rolls of that one cabildo you can find the roots for most of the ramas that exist today.

Many ilés reflect the balance of power of the old cabildos. They are jointly headed by a babalawo and an apetebí who is also a santera, with the babalawo in charge of the Ifá ceremonies and the apetebí in charge of Ocha ceremonies and initiations. The apetebí is the babalawo's most valuable assistant and is the joint administrator of the ilé. That way the ilé oricha becomes a closed calabash with Ifá and Ocha, male and female being properly represented.

Besides having the gift of the ability to produce a life many women have another gift babalawos will never experience. Women have the ability of having an oricha come from the Other World and inhabit their body physically for a time. The majority of horses, or someone who is ridden or possessed by an oricha, are women. Something Orula does not permit his priests to experience. In Ifá virtually everything that surrounds Orula is female. In the oddun Irete Meyi we find the traditional salute to Ifá and his priests: *"Iború, Iboya, Ibocheché."* This is translated to "sacrifice offered, sacrifice accepted, sacrifice is blessed," which was originally the names of the three women who saved Orunmila after falling into a pit, while the *apere* (receptacle) in which Orula lives is considered female as well.

In Lucumí Ifá the apetebí is considered to be the babalawo's right hand, and she has access to places and ceremonies closed to all except for babalawos. They are also in charge of much of what goes on during the ceremonies. The apetebí is also considered senior to any of the men who have received abo faca by virtue of having gone through certain ceremonies, which the men do not. During any Ifá ceremony, the apetebí is in charge of everything outside of the room where the babalawos are working, and her word is law. In fact, the apetebí is the only non-babalawo who is directly saluted by babalawos by saying, *"Apetebí iború, apetebí iboya, apetebí ibocheché."*[1]

In Afro-Cuban Ifá, the apetebí is absolutely necessary for the initiation of a new babalawo. There are ceremonies that must be performed by the apetebí, including one so crucial that without it the initiation is not complete, and the would-be initiate cannot become a babalawo. There is also an added benefit. In gratitude for her indispensable help Orunmila adds ten years to the life of the apetebí who performs this ceremony.

The woman who performs these ceremonies, traditionally the initiate's wife, also becomes part owner of the new initiate's Ifá. This means that she can never be refused access to that Ifá under any circumstances, as well as other things. This fact has led some babalawos to have their mothers perform these ceremonies out of fear of a break up. If there is a divorce the former wife can walk right up and complain about the spouses to their own Ifá and there's nothing that can be done.

One Ekin or Sixteen?

In a number of traditional African lines women receive sixteen ekin nuts in their kofá as opposed to traditional Lucumí Ifá where the woman receives one or two ekin nuts depending on her sign. Some neo-traditionalists feel this is an expression of Cuban machismo and misogyny, but the practice of giving women a single ekin called Ekó Ifá (often shortened to Ekofá or Kofá) was prevalent in Africa as late as 1899, as described by the Yoruba author James Johnson. Therefore, there is no question that our practice of giving one ekin has a history in Africa. The fact of the matter is, Ifá is Ifá, whether you have one ekin or a hundred. The important thing is that Ifá will hear.

On the other hand, there is a little-known ceremony where an apetebí receives a full hand of sixteen ekins, and it is one of the most beautiful ceremonies in Ifá. Called *Adele Wa Ni Ifá Tolú*, the ceremony elevates the apetebí to the status of *apetebí ayafá* (wife of Ifá), which is the highest level a woman can reach in Ifá. During this initiation she receives all sixteen ekin nuts and a new oddun defining her life destiny, which supersedes the oddun from her kofá.[2] At this point she can and should learn more about Ifá's oddduns. Many ayafás exhibit an impressive amount of knowledge about the oddduns, although she still cannot divine with the ekines or ecuele. In fact, the apetebí ayafa can even use the ecuele if her husband or child is ill. Only an apetebí who has performed the ceremonies to complete a new babalawo's initiation is eligible to have this ceremony performed. It is a truly beautiful ceremony that I am not allowed to discuss with anyone except babalawos or apetebí ayafás.

In the United States, there are people who have come to the mistaken conclusion that apetebís are servants to the babalawos. There is one website claiming the word ayafá means slave of Ifá. Apparently this website has their own dialect of Lucumí or Yoruba, as Ayá means wife in both languages, and as many of the most famous and powerful olorichas in the history of the religion were also apetebís, this is a conclusion that defies belief. For instance, indisputably the two most powerful santeras in Havana, Latuán, and Efunché were both married to babalawos and were their apetebí Ayafas. Latuán was married to the great babalawo Bernabé Menocal (Baba Eyiogbe), and Efunché was married to the babalawo Jacinto Fernandez (Kaindé). Efunché and Latuán were so powerful nobody worked in the religion without their approval. The idea that these two olorichas, who utterly dominated Havana, would be subservient to anyone is laughable at best. Aurora Lamar (Obatolá), who is the root of what is by far the largest rama of the Lucumí religion, was married to a babalawo as well.[3] What's worse, to imply these santeras were subservient slaves to their babalawo husbands is extremely demeaning toward these women. In fact, the babalawos' tendency to marry powerful women rather than fear them might point to a healthy attitude toward women that was probably rare in the late 1800s.

The apetebí ayafá, carrying Orunmila, leads the babalawos into the Ifá ceremonial room on the day of the Itá. During the Itá she carries the ekines to the babalawo who is seated in preparation to divine with them. At the end of the ceremony she dances the ekines out of the room carrying them on her head at the head of the procession.

Despite all of this the role of women is also one of the most misunderstood subjects in Afro-Cuban Ifá with accusations of misogyny and sexism laid at the feet not only of babalawos but of Ifá itself. While unfortunately sexist babalawos exist Ifá itself is anything but sexist in nature. Where does this perception come from and how much truth is there to the charges leveled against Ifá? Much of the confusion surrounding the perceived sexism of Afro-Cuban Ifá has been caused by the aftermath of the apparently modern practice of initiating women as iyanifás in some parts of Yorubaland. The prohibition against this practice is often held up as evidence of an inherent sexism in Afro-Cuban Ifá, particularly by practitioners of present-day African traditions in the United States, with some even claiming the prohibition is a purely Cuban invention. Is this true? First let's look at why we have this prohibition in the first place.

In the oddun Oché Yekún, Orula states unequivocally that Odun must be present for a person to be initiated as a babalawo and that without her presence Ifá will not recognize them as a babalawo and the person will have accomplished nothing. Below is an excerpt from the African version:

> If one wishes to become a babalawo,
> He must enter Odun's grove.
> But if he does not first propitiate Odun in her Apere (receptacle)
> He will accomplish nothing.
> Ifá will not know that the person has come to be initiated as a babalawo.
> Orunmila will not recognize his child.[4]

This is why traditional Lucumí babalawos do not recognize anyone who has not been initiated in Odun's presence as an Ifá priest. Therefore, women cannot be initiated as Ifá priests because Odun prohibits women from being in her presence. This is due to the cruel treatment she received from the first women she encountered when she came to this world. Following is another excerpt from the African version of this pataki:

> Because Odun is the babalawo's power.
> Ifá says, if the babalawo possesses Ifá, he must have come before Odun.
> The power that Odun gives him says that.
> No woman must look upon her form.
> From this day no babalawo is complete without Odun.

Anyone initiated without propitiating Odun
in Igbodún will not be able to consult Ifá.

As you can see, the babalawo is nothing without the primordial feminine power Odun/Olófin as she is the ultimate source of all of the babalawos' power. Lucumí babalawos will not consider violating Odun's prohibitions for she is not only powerful but also extremely dangerous when offended. The absolute necessity for her presence at the consecration of an Ifá priest led Cuba's first babalawo, Adechina, to risk life and limb to travel back to Africa and return to Cuba so he could bring her back to the island as we discussed earlier. For Lucumí babalawos the initiation of anyone as an Ifá priest without Odun being present is considered an offense to Odun and to the immense sacrifices made by our ancestors as well.

What does history say about the initiation of iyanifá in Africa? There are claims that iyanifás have been around for hundreds, if not thousands, of years. If that's the case we should have little trouble finding records of their existence among the numerous sources who have documented Ifá in Yorubaland over the last two hundred years. As it turns out just the opposite is true.

Dr. William Bascom, universally recognized as the foremost academic authority on Ifá in the twentieth century, also stated that only men can become babalawo. During his extensive field studies in twelve different cities he never encountered or heard of a single female Ifá priest acting as a diviner. Numerous sources from Yorubaland going back to the early to mid-nineteenth century clearly state that only men could become Ifá diviners, and none mention women Ifá diviners. In fact, there is no source mentioning the existence of Iyanifás in Yorubaland before the 1970s.

In 1992, the king of the South Carolinian Oyotunji African Village, Adefunmi, was pressured by the women of Oyotunji to be initiated as Ifá priests in Dahomey, in spite of the fact that Adefunmi's credentials as Obá came from the Yoruba spiritual capital of Ifé. This was because the babalawos in Ifé still refused to initiate women at the time.[5] Since then, Ifé appears to have begun initiating women as Ifá priests.

Over the years I have come to the conclusion that the iyanifá likely came into existence due to the extremely destructive effects colonialism had upon the traditional religions in Yorubaland. For more than a hundred years Christians or Muslims, who will not allow traditional practitioners to attend, have run most of the schools in Yorubaland. For generations children have been taught that the rich culture and spirituality of the traditional religions are merely bush religions consisting of nothing more than a jumbled mass of ignorant superstitions. This led to a steep decline in the traditional religions in Yorubaland, and along with that came the fear that the knowledge and traditions of Ifá would be completely lost. This may very well have led babalawos who, lacking any male children willing to spend the years of training necessary to become babalawos, began to look to training their female children in desperation.

The view that if a woman can't be a babalawo then she must be accepting a subservient role propounded by these neo-traditionalists has led to a lot of the misunderstandings and accusations of misogyny we see today. Another source of these issues is simply jealousy. An apetebí is often shown more respect, and has more power and knowledge than many of her non-apetebí elders even though she may have less seniority than them. Anyone who looks around them can see that the natural order of things is a balance of power between male and female, with neither one being superior. From the closed calabash that contains the universe itself, to the closed calabash of the ilé oricha jointly administered by the babalawo and the oloricha apetebí.

Apetebí iború, Apetebí iboya, Apetebí ibocheché.

Chapter Twelve
Tata Gaitán

Ochossi was a hunter dedicated to trapping and hunting for the other orichas, but they never gave him anything in return. This situation continued until one day Oshossi decided to go to Orula, who told him he should travel to another town and work as a blacksmith. Ochossi went to this other town and worked for a week before Ogún saw him and took Ochossi on as an apprentice. After a while Ochossi went to another town and learned another trade. He went from town to town in this way, learning various trades, and came to know quite a lot about everything.

Then one day it happened that Olófin began to look for someone to be king of a great kingdom. As the word spread, many knowledgeable and wise people came to Olófin in hopes of becoming king, but even the wisest and most knowledgeable knew a lot about only one or two things. Only Ochossi knew a bit about everything, so Olófin made him king.

"Each of us is as Obatalá made us, but what we become is up to us."

The batá drums usually used to salute the orichas stop and a new set of drums is brought out to thunder forth. They are the drums specially consecrated for Olokun, the powerful oricha who rules the depths of the ocean.

On New Year's Day 1943 a dancer advances forward wearing burlap and her dress covers her so not one bit of flesh is seen, with huge breasts formed from bundles of rags that bounce when she walks or dances. The priestesses surrounding her cover her with finely decorated burlap shawls and cover the floor where she steps with fine silks befitting her royalty for this is Sumúgagá of Olokun's royal court. Sumúgagá, whose name alludes to her enormous breasts, fertility, and the ability to nourish the world, is surrounded by twenty-one elder priestesses dancing around her with cupped hands under their breasts. Another dancer advances wearing the mask of the daunting oricha Olokun himself. Dancing the mask of Olokun is Tata Gaitán. He is the obá of the religion in Cuba and the most knowledgeable priest, especially regarding Olokun's secrets. For the other babalawos performing the ceremony the joy of the event is tempered by the knowledge that a babalawo is expected to die soon after a Dance of Olokun's Masks is performed. But nobody would have ever guessed that this time it would be Tata Gaitán himself who would be the one to die after dancing the masks and that this would be the last time Olokun's masks would ever be danced in Cuba.

The legendary Tata Gaitán (1861—1944), whose full name was Eulogio Rodriguez Gaitán (Ogundá Fun), was not only one of the most famous and powerful babalawos to have ever lived but he was the only person ever installed as the obá, ruling over the entire Lucumí religious community in Cuba. He is considered the root of the rama of Ifá I belong to, even though it is properly a sub-branch of the Adechina branch of Ifá.[1]

Not only was Tata Gaitán a great babalawo, but he was a very powerful and feared palero in the Bantu religion of Palo Mayombe. Practitioners there could use the enchained spirits of their ngangas for any purpose according to their will. Commonly known by the nickname Tata, which is the title given to palo priests, he was more than capable of defending himself against all comers. He was also a member of the ultra-secret Abakua Society from the Calabarí region of Africa, whose ancestors were said to have had the ability to change into leopards. Gaitán was not initiated as a santero and received his orichas before passing to Ifá. This is not uncommon for children of the warrior orichas Elegguá, Ogún, and Ochossi. Despite the fact he had only *santos lavados* or washed orichas (had received the orichas without actually being initiated as an oloricha), he was known to have mastered every aspect of both Ocha and Ifá. Hundreds of people in ilés from all parts of Cuba had the good fortune of his participation at their initiation as a santero. Despite the fact that some now claim a babalawo must be initiated as an oloricha to work in the initiation of an oricha priest, this is not traditionally the case. There is no oddun that supports such a notion and neither Adechina or Tata Gaitán were ever denied entrance to any ceremony even though they were not initiated as santeros first. Despite that fact the vast majority of babalawos make Ocha first, and unless Ifá says otherwise, my advice is to always be initiated in Ocha first rather than skipping steps.

The African-born Oluguere in Camaguey initiated Tata Gaitán as a babalawo in the early 1880s with his grandfather in Ifá, Adechina, serving as his oyugbona. Unfortunately, Tata Gaitán was able to train with his Oluguere for only a few years as his padrino decided to return to Africa only to die in Mexico during the attempt. Before Oluguere left he sent the young Gaitán to his brother in Ifá Ño Blas Cárdenas to continue his training. Ño Akonkó Oluguere and Ño Blas Cárdenas were among the first to be initiated to Ifá by Adéchina on Cuban soil even though both Oluguere and Cárdenas had been brought from Africa as slaves. They both shared the oddun in Ifá Oyekún Meji as well.[2]

Tata Gaitán first had to find the mysterious Ño Cárdenas. All he knew was that Ño Cárdenas was thought to be living in seclusion somewhere in the Matanzas area. Armed with only a special prayer for the Ifá oddun shared by his padrino and his mentor-to-be he searched high and low, near and far, with no results. Finally he came upon an old santera who knew Ño Cárdenas, and although Tata Gaitán was a stranger to her she gave him precise directions to the remote cave where he had hidden himself. When Gaitán arrived at the cave Ño Cárdenas demanded to know who he was and why he had come. Tata Gaitán responded by prostrating himself at the feet of his elder and reciting the prayer taught to him by his padrino Oluguery. Ño Cárdenas immediately recognized it as the prayer Oyekún Meji taught to him and Oluguere by their padrino Adechina. Eulogio further explained to his elder that he was the godchild of Oluguery who had directed him to seek Ño Cárdenas before leaving for Africa. Satisfied that Tata Gaitán was who and what he said he was, the older babalawo asked the young babalawo to sit in the cave and rest, and he would begin teaching him after he was rested. Ño Cárdenas was curious how Tata Gaitán was able to find his cave, and the young babalawo told him about the old santera who had given him such detailed directions.

"She talks too much," Ño Cárdenas responded curtly. A few days later, the old santera was dead.

After the thorough grilling Tata Gaitán was accepted as Ño Cárdenas's pupil and was able to continue his training with the elder. He taught the young babalawo the songs, the prayers, and hundreds of ceremonies. The young Eulogio had such exceptional intelligence that he was soon well on his way to becoming a great master of ceremonies. After training with Ño Cárdenas for a number of years, Tata Gaitán went back to train further with his oyugbona Adechina. In the time-honored fashion, Tata Gaitán cared for the elderly Adechina washing his feet and grooming him. Always eager to learn and willing to apply himself to the tasks no matter how long or difficult he became known for his profound knowledge of Ifá and particularly for his exceptional knowledge of the secrets of Olokun, the powerful oricha of the bottom of the sea. In fact, Gaitán was credited with being the first Cuban-born babalawo with knowledge of how to dance Olokun's masks, and with his death he became the last.

The feeding of Olokun in the middle of the sea and the dancing of Olokun's masks was an exceptionally delicate and dangerous ceremony. So much so that a babalawo was expected to die every time the masks were danced. If any mistakes were made during Olokun's masked dance, or sacred objects fell to the ground, it would spell disaster not only for the dancer but for the community as well. This fear is taken very seriously by the babalawos who are old enough to know. In 1958, the letter of the year was Ofún Nalbe in osogbo with Olokun ruling over the year. Olokun was demanding that the babalawos dance her masks in order to appease the hot-tempered and dangerous oricha. The babalawos were so afraid that they spent hours finding an alternative offering that Olokun would accept instead of dancing the masks. Finally they succeeded.

This was a particularly delicate situation as the oddun Ofún Nalbe warns that many people will die from guns fired in acts of vengeance. The oddun also warns of war and confrontations, especially those sparked by economic issues. Ofun Nalbe advises any new government to avoid taking on the vices of the previous one. Of course, we now know that Ifá was predicting the upcoming success of the Cuban Revolution. In fact, the oddun for 1959 Baba Eyiogbe whose proverb "A King Dies, A New King is Crowned," clearly refers to Bautista being replaced by Castro as a response for not listening to the people, although in this instance he did not actually die. In that case Ifá's prediction came to pass within one day.

At the end of the 1800s, the first Apertura del Año/Letra del Año (Opening of the Year/Letter of the Year) ceremonies were first performed in Cuba. Now the Letter of the Year Ceremony, where babalawos from all parts of the world gather to learn what the new year will bring, is one of the most awaited events in the santeros year. However, for all of the prophecies for the year by far the most important part of the ceremonies is the Opening of the Year Ceremony, which precedes this divination. These special ceremonies performed directly to the various positions of nature as well as the orichas and the eggun were all performed to ensure well-being for the community and the world. At the close of the nineteenth century the ceremony was performed for the first time at the Cabildo Africano Lucumí. Adechina (Obara Meyi), Oluguere (Oyekun Meyi), the famous drum creator Olu Aña Marcos García Ifálolá (Baba Eyiogbe), Tata Gaitán (Ogundá Fun), Bernardo Rojas (Irete Untedi), and José Carmen Baitista (Ogbe Weñe) were the babalawos who helped accomplish this.

In 1902, due to Adechina's health problems Tata Gaitán had to take over directing the Letter of the Year Ceremony. In addition to the babalawos mentioned above they now had the aid of Secundino Crucet (Osalo Fobeyó), Bernabé Menocál (Baba Ejiogbe), Quintín Lecón García (Oturaniko), and José Asunción Villalonga (Ogundamasa). When Adechina died in 1906, Tata Gaitán had Bernardo Rojas direct the ceremony under his tutelage. The last Opening of the Year Ceremony during that time was held at Bernardo Rojas's house in 1959 shortly before his death on May 9 was directed by Joaquín Salazar, and wasn't held again until 1962.

In 1910, Tata Gaitán became the only person to ever be consecrated as obá of the religion in Cuba receiving the titles Ashedá and Araba in the process. Ashedá is the name of Orunmila's first disciple and Araba is the largest and most sacred tree in the religion. Araba is also the title of the head of all babalawos in Ilé Ifé. No one on the island had ever had this honor bestowed on them before or since. Presided over by the African-born babalawo José Asunción Villalonga, head of his own Ifá lineage, the ceremony must have been impressive and Eulogio Gaitán is said to have ridden across the entire city mounted on a pure white horse as part of the rite. Tata Gaitán was not the eldest babalawo in Cuba but became recognized as the most knowledgeable one through his hard work and in following the example of his oddun. He became exceptionally well versed in many aspects of the Afro-Cuban religions, so in the end Tata Gaitán became a king in much the same way as Ochossi did in the itán that began this chapter.

In 1916, Tata Gaitán bought a mansion at 35 Palo Blanco in a well-to-do area of Guanabacoa, Cuba. Palo Blanco wasn't the original street name, but was taken from the phrase Pa' Lo' Blanco, translated to Para Los Blancos, meaning "For Whites Only." It was named this with the intention to warn away blacks from this exclusively white part of town during the time of Spanish dominance. The street is now named Aranguren.

Having headed one of the greatest institutions in the history of the Lucumí as vice president Tata Gaitán used the experience, training, and knowledge to operate his own home under the same principles of mutual aid to the Lucumí community that had guided the great cabildos. Tata Gaitán turned his palatial home into a community center with an open-door policy where he took care of his elder babalawos and young babalawos who often traveled hundreds of miles to train under him. He also looked after his neighbor's children, local street kids, and even the nuns from the local parish. He helped just about anybody who came to him for aid and assistance. Tata Gaitán became the subject of a popular hit song in the 1930s *Un Brujo en Guanabacoa* (A Wizard in Guanabacoa) popularized by Abelardo Barroso and others about an imagined visit to a babalawo.

Tata Gaitán died in 1944 shortly after dancing the masks of Olokun, and for years no babalawo attempted to dance the masks out of fear they too might die if they made a mistake. The babalawo's death was a big event in Cuba, with the largest papers like *El Crisol* and *El Alerta* carrying the story. It is said that shortly before he died Tata Gaitán asked his ahijados to sever his head and bury it separately so other paleros wouldn't be able to use his skull to make an nganga and enslave his spirit. Tata Gaitán had good reason to be concerned. The bones and spirit of such a fearless and accomplished tata would have been a real prize.

Tata Gaitán (Ogundá Fun)
Photo provided courtesy of David Brown

Epilogue: One Babalawo's Story

I am a babalawo from the Tata Gaitán rama of Lucumí Ifá.[1,2] Although there are a few different branches, Lucumí Ifá is one because all of our lines intermingle and are virtually identical to one other. Lineage is more a matter of pedigree than practice.

It was more curiosity than anything that led me to the appointment with the babalawo at the *botanica* (Santería supply store) near the apartment in San Francisco's Mission District where I lived. Although I didn't know what to expect during the consultation, I certainly did not expect the events that would occur that afternoon. Events that would turn my life upside down and change my life completely.

On the day of the appointment I was greeted by a short, effusive man who introduced himself as simply Pete and I was ushered to the back office where the consultation would occur. After a series of prayers Pete threw an ecuele onto the little mat on his desk. He looked at the sign and then gave me a piercing look, saying only "Hmmmm." He then handed me a stone and a shell, telling me to shake them in my hands and separate them, one in each hand. He threw the chain twice more and asked for my left hand, which held the stone. He then told me the sign had come in something called iré, which meant I had come on the positive side of the sign. He then followed this with a number of questions, each time repeating the process of having me shake and separate the stone and the shell and then throwing twice and writing in his notebook. Finally, he seemed to be satisfied with the results of his questions and began to speak, starting nearly everything he said with the words "Ifá says…"

"This is the oddun or sign where the Table of Ifá was born, and Ifá says you were born to be a babalawo. You have to become a high priest in this religion, like me. Ifá says you were practicing Ifá in heaven before you were born, but we'll need to confirm all this when you receive your abo faca. The abo faca is the first initiation in Ifá for men."

He paused and then began to tell me things about myself that nobody else knew—I mean nobody. Orula was talking about things that even my best friend never knew. It was as if Ifá was saying to me, "In case you have doubts about any of this," or perhaps Orula was trying to rattle me. If that was the case, it worked. After the consultation I had to walk around the Mission District streets for over an hour to settle my nerves.

He told me that in the meantime I should receive my elekes,[3] which he described as like a baptism into the religion. He then told his wife, a priestess of Ochún and apetebí to prepare a set of necklaces for Obatalá. It was a lot for me to process. I had gone for a simple consultation only to be told that I was to become a high priest in a strange religion I really knew little about. I later discovered Pete Rivera was the first babalawo in San Francisco. I had managed to stumble on the only babalawo in the entire city, and I had been living just one block away from his shop for years. Little did I know at the time that this man would become like a second father to me and would guide and shape my spiritual life.

I received my necklaces a few weeks after the consultation. At the end of the ceremony I saluted my new godparents for the first time. First I saluted my new madrina, throwing myself level on the floor with my hands at my sides followed by crossing my arms across my chest and asking for her blessings. Then padrino taught me how to salute a babalawo by leaning forward and touching the floor with my right hand and saying, "Oluwo iború, Oluwo Iboya, Oluwo Ibocheché."

Then padrino wrote the words down and handed it to me, saying, "A short pencil is better than the longest memory."

That night as I slept I had a particularly vivid dream. It was incredibly clear. If anything it was clearer and more vivid than in my waking life. In my dream I was in a cave with a large group of santeros all dressed impeccably in white. They were all saluting me as if I were a babalawo saying, "Iború, Iboya, Ibocheché." Who were these people and why were they saluting me? The dream was so intense and confusing that I went the very next day to the botanica to ask about it. Padrino Pete told me the santeros in my dream were egguns and that in Africa they used to bury people in caves before they buried people in the ground. But why were they saluting me like that? I wasn't even a santero much less a babalawo?

Padrino Pete shot back, "Don't you remember what Ifá told you? He said you were practicing Ifá before you even came to this world. It will be very interesting to see what Ifá says when you receive your abo faca." In the meantime, I didn't need the paper Padrino Pete had given me anymore. The salute to a babalawo had been burned into my soul in that dream.

It was almost a year before Padrino Pete was able to organize the first abo faca and kofá ceremonies in San Francisco on August 8, 1988. As there weren't that many babalawos in the US at the time, padrino had to fly babalawos in from all over the country for the ceremony. It was confirmed there that I was to make Ifá and learned that my oricha was Obatalá. I am an oluwo, a term commonly used for a babalawo who is initiated first as an iworo or santero before passing on to Ifá. I had been encouraged by my godparents to take my time and to learn before getting initiated so it was four years before I was initiated as a santero. I made Obatalá in San Francisco on August 17, 1991, and had the great good fortune of receiving much of my in-depth training from my oyugbona, the famous Cuban oriaté Guillermo Diago (Obá Bí). At the time of my initiation he already had more than fifty years as a priest of Changó under his belt. I was thrilled on the third day of my initiation when Obatalá gave me the name of Efún Muyiwá through shell divination. I had been given the honor of receiving the name of the oriaté who had directed Padrino Guillermo's own initiation. In 1995 I made

Ifá in Havana, Cuba, and all of my subsequent initiations were performed there as well even though Padrino Pete himself had been initiated to Ifá in the United States.

Typically you make Ifá in the place your padrino was initiated but the death of Pete's padrino changed everything. Pete's padrino, who was also my grandfather in Ifá Domingo Sanchez (Ogbe Che), had an oddun prohibiting him from carrying firearms. The night my grandfather violated that prohibition was the night he died. Domingo had received a distressed phone call in the middle of the night telling him that his business was being broken into. Domingo instinctively grabbed his revolver and rushed to his store and ended up facing tragic consequences. Members of the mafia gunned him down in the street outside his business. Because of the mob connections the babalawos were too frightened to attend the *itutu* (memorial ceremony) traditionally performed on priests who have passed away.

My Padrino Pete, who had less than a year in Ifá since his initiation, was forced to perform the itutu on the bullet-pierced corpse of his godfather alone via continuous phone calls to his elders during the ceremony. Padrino Pete told me later that he could feel the bullet hole as he held his dead padrino's head to perform the ceremonies. The ceremony was finally completed to the orichas' satisfaction and it will always be to Padrino Pete's credit that he was afraid of nothing and no one when it came to performing his responsibilities to Ifá.

Although my Padrino Pete made his Ifá in the United States my Ifá initiation was performed in Havana because Pete wanted to make absolutely sure the initiation was performed to the highest standards possible. Also, tradition dictates that the first person a babalawo initiates should be performed at the hands of one's own padrino. In his case, because his own padrino Domingo Sanchez had died my Padrino Pete opted to fulfill this obligation with his grandfather in Ifá Erminio Ogbe Funfunlo in Cuba. Because the Ifá was arranged in Havana by my great-grandfather in Cuba who was ninety years old, almost all the babalawos working the ceremony were elders. The only exception was the obá who would direct my initiation as master of ceremonies. This obá, Miguelito Perez (Ogbe Dandy), only had five years as a babalawo at the time and was the youngest babalawo there. He may have been young but he had been raised around Ifá, and he had been surrounded by Ifá priests from the time he was born. I remember thinking at first about how young the obá was, but any doubts to his abilities disappeared as I listened to the oluwos discussing the upcoming ceremonies. When it came to knowledge of Ifá, this babalawo was simply in a different league than anyone I had ever seen. In a short time I realized why he was the obvious choice to perform the ceremonies. Later, when there was a falling out between my padrino and Erminio (Ogbe Funfunló), Padrino Miguelito became my oyugbona for the rest of my initiations. Finally, when Padrino Pete became too ill to teach it fell upon Padrino Miguelito to take over the role of training me in my padrino's name as well. Later I received Odun (Olófin) and Orí from Miguelito as well.

Miguelito Perez Alvarez has shown endless patience to me over the years, answering my ceaseless barrage of questions, taking me under his wing, and making sure I have the proper fundamento when working Ifá. He is an endless source of knowledge and wisdom, and for me epitomizes what it means to be a great babalawo.

Although Padrino Pete may not have as much technical knowledge as Padrino Miguelito he made up for it in aché, the mysterious power that fills the universe and makes things happen. He always just knew what cleansing or offering would be needed, and with him even the plainest ceremonies were always enormously effective. When I think of the amazing amount of aché Padrino Pete has I am often reminded of a story about Miguel Febles (Odí Ka), which the Havana babalawos like to relate ... and debate.

One day Miguel Febles was with Fran Cabrera and said to him, "The babalawos think that everything is just throwing the ecuele and nothing more, but you also have to divine using your aché."

"That's spiritism not Ifá," Fran responded.

"No, it is not spiritism, it is Ifá."

At that moment a man passed by who was a complete stranger to both of them. Febles said to the man, "You have thirty-three pesos and twenty-two centavos in your pocket," and then asked the man to check his pockets. When the man emptied his pockets he had exactly thirty-three pesos and twenty-two centavos, not a centavo more or less.

Pete Rivera always had an amazing amount of aché. I don't know how many times he would call for something during an itá or consultation and the elder babalawos would say, "No, no, no. That's not correct," and would talk about how Padrino Pete's suggestion didn't fit the oddun.

Padrino, who never lets anything hold him back, would simply say, "Ask Orula." Sure enough Orula would confirm what padrino said. Padrino Pete was like a father to me and one of the greatest things he ever taught me was how to work with aché, and that if you know how to work aché you don't have to do anything big or complex to achieve tremendous results. It just has to be the right thing, at the right time, in the right way. That lesson is a priceless gift to me.

One day a woman asked me to help her quit shooting drugs. She had tried everything to no avail.

"I don't want to die," she told me.

I told her I would take her situation up with Obatalá. I simply lit a candle to the oricha and talked to him in ways I knew Obatalá appreciates. Later that night, when she tried to shoot her drugs she began to vomit continuously. She spent the rest of the night throwing up, but quit shooting drugs.

About a year later she slipped. After shooting the drugs she began to feel an incredible amount of pain in her neck. After a week of nonstop pain she went to a doctor who told her she had incurable arthritis so we went back to Obatalá. She had to quit and never attempt to do the drugs again or she would pay a heavy price. She agreed. Sure enough, the pain was gone the next day, and when she went back to see the doctor there was no arthritis to be found. She never shot drugs again.

One day while chatting with a few other olorichas and babalawos I brought up the story. One santera's response was, "If you can do all that with a (bleeping) candle, I'm afraid of you." Of course it wasn't the candle and it wasn't me. It was Obatalá and aché.

Maferefún Obatalá (Obatalá be praised)! Moducué Padrino Pete (I thank you Padrino Pete)!

The problem with relying on aché alone is if you are not careful you can deplete your aché and have serious problems where even your health can be affected. On the other hand, if you concentrate too much on complex ceremonies and rituals they can be unsuccessful if they lack aché. As in all things in this world, there must be a balance.

Padrino Miguelito has accumulated a tremendous amount of knowledge over the years and he has been kind enough to share a few grains of that knowledge with me. One of the things I cherish most is that each time I am in Havana Padrino Miguelito and I burn the midnight oil talking Ifá until two or three o'clock in the morning when we realize how late it is and that we must get at least an hour or two of sleep before the next day's activities. He is a bottomless font of wisdom and knowledge, and it is through his teachings that I have realized the true depth and profundity that is Ifá. He has also given me a vast arsenal of weapons and tools that I can use in virtually any situation to aid my family, godchildren, and all those who come to Ifá for help in their lives. Moducué Padrino Miguelito!

Between my padrinos Pete and Miguelito I feel I have received the perfect balance between working aché and the more recondite and technical aspects of Ifá. These two more than anyone else have helped me to fulfill my lifelong dream of learning the secrets of the universe. Moducué Padrino Pete and Padrino Miguelito.

All the things I have been taught by my elders, both in Cuba and in the United States, has given me a depth and perspective on the religion I could not have gained in any other way. For this I am thankful to my padrinos and all the elders and the younger babalawos in both countries that I have had the honor to work with.

To Pete Rivera (Odí Ogundá), Miguelito Perez (Ogbe Dandy), Julito Collazo (Iwori Kosó) in Ifá and Guillermo Diago (Obá Bí-Ibaé) in Ocha. It has been my great fortune to have been blessed with the best padrinos a person can ever hope for. Maferefún Elegguá, Maferefún Orula, Maferefún Obatalá, Maferefún Changó.

My Padrino in Ifá, Pete Rivera

My oyugbona in Ifá, Miguelito Perez Alvarez (Ogbe Dandy),
with me and my family, Central Havana, Cuba

Notes

Notes on the Writing of This Book

1. The Anagó or Lucumí language used in Santería was formed from a number of dialects, particularly those of Oyó and Egbado. The Yoruba tones have been lost, but are sometimes approximated with the accents borrowed from the Spanish language. Words are spelled phonetically according to the Spanish orthography, so often several different spellings can be seen for the same word. I attempted to use some of the more common spellings of words without falling into using pseudo-Yoruba spellings that fail to represent how the language is actually used in either Cuba or Yorubaland. In this book I have also used the spelling "oddun" when speaking of the Ifá signs, and "Odun" when talking about the Supreme Being. Although they are usually spelled identically, I used this form to make it easier for the reader to differentiate between the two. A well-researched work that explores this subject is *Anagó* by Maria "Oggun Gbemi" Concordia.

Introduction

1. Samuel Johnson's *History of Yoruba* places Ifá as being present at the founding of the Yoruba religious capital of Ilé Ifé with evidence of habitation going back as far as the sixth century BCE. But, on the

other hand, oral traditions state that Ifá divination may be more than eight thousand years old.

2. While the patakís and refránes themselves are not considered secret, many traditional Lucumí babalawos, including myself and my god-fathers who initiated me, refrain from publicly stating which oddun the histories and sayings are associated with, so this information is for the exclusive use of fully initiated Ifá priests who have the aché and authority from Olófin to interpret or work Ifá. This is to prevent further misuse of the information by those who have not been properly consecrated as babalawos. Exceptions are of course made when the context demands it, such as during divination or to illustrate the influence of a particular oddun in a person's life.

Chapter One: What Is Ifá?

1. Ulli Beir gives an accurate description of the view most of us have regarding faith and belief in his book *Return of the Gods: The Sacred Art of Suzanne Wenger.*

2. In fact, we often refer to people as the omo of their patron orichas. For example, "Emiliano is an omo Obatalá."

3. Quoted from *Santeria: The Religion: Faith, Rites and Magic* by Migene Gonzáles-Wippler.

Chapter Two: How Ifá Works

1. This famous proverb comes from a patakí where a hunter went to Orula and was warned that not sacrificing his hunt could lead to his death. The hunter not only refused to perform the sacrifice, but he openly mocked Orula. The hunter returned with his catch, which included porcupines, and held a big dinner to further humiliate Orula. But during the dinner he accidentally swallowed one of the porcupine's spines, which got caught deep in his throat, and within a few minutes the hunter bled out and died. Upon hearing of the tragic dinner, the babalawos merely remarked, "Orula's word never falls to the floor." Unfortunately, this proverb has become an exam-

ple of the misuse of Ifá books by non-babalawos as I have seen where again the oricha in the proverb has been changed from Orula to another oricha. Besides the obvious issues that come with changing the oricha, the proverb does not make sense in the context of the parable from which the saying originated.

Chapter Three: Babalawo

1. *The Anagó Language of Cuba* by Maria Oggun Gbemim Concordia is an expansion of her Master's thesis taking the position that the Anagó language is not a corrupted form of the Yoruba language, but a separate language that evolved from the various ethnic groups and their experience in Cuba in much the same way as the Lucumí religion did as a whole.

2. For years, we heard reports from Africa that all learning occurred there before initiation into Ifá. But later, we found that at least in certain parts of Yoruba country, the practice is very similar to Cuba where a person must be initiated as an Ifá priest before learning the secrets of the odduns. The secrecy surrounding the odduns seems to be the traditional approach, and in the 1930s and 1950s William Bascom encountered strong opposition to recording the verses throughout Yorubaland as they were considered professional secrets. This attitude appears to have been far-ranging as Bascom's research was conducted heavily in Ilé Ifé, Oyó, and Meko, and he spent time in about a dozen other towns throughout Yorubaland in Nigeria. It is possible that as the traditional Yoruba religions became more and more endangered by colonialism and the encroachment of Christianity and Islam, they may have loosened these restrictions in order to prevent the loss of verses.

3. Pichardo, Ernesto. From Pichardo's press release posted to his social community site (diasporaorishanetwork.yuku.com/topic/894/Lukum-ifa-book-unveiled-and-authenticated) said that he had acquired two copies of *Iwe ni Iyewó ni Ifá Orunmila*, which he was turning over to the Africana Knowledge Group of South Florida that he helped to

found. Later, when this Working Group apparently floundered, Pichardo reclaimed the copies of the book.

4. The preface with the disclosure that three copies of the book had fallen into the hands of three non-babalawos and the subsequent measures he took to prevent a reoccurrence of the event is taken from a copy of the second edition of *Iwe ni Iyewó ni Ifá Orunmila* in the author's possession.

5. I intend to release this second edition of *Iwe ni Iyewó ni Ifá Orunmila*, which is the probable source of the information in many of the various *Dice Ifás* published later. The book will be first published in Spanish and later in an English translation. In the spirit of the original versions, the book will only be made available to babalawos.

6. I am hoping to be successful in my attempts to acquire a copy of the earliest version of the book in the near future. If I do succeed, I will try to release the version of this book in Spanish and in an English translation. They will be sold under the same conditions as with *Iwe ni Iyewó ni Ifá Orunmila*, in that it will only be sold to babalawos.

Chapter Four: Ifá Comes to Cuba

1. In this book the patakís and refránes are not associated with the oddun they are from, except in special cases such as where they are being used to illustrate how a particular babalawo's life matched the predictions of their oddun. This is the traditional attitude in Cuba and appears to have been traditional in Africa until fairly recently as well. My padrinos Pete Rivera (Odí Ogundá) in San Francisco and Miguelito Perez (Ogbe Dandy) in Cuba follow this tradition, as do I. The abuses of this knowledge by non-babalawos who gained access to books on Ifá intended for the exclusive use of babalawos confirms the wisdom of these measures. One particularly grievous example occurred when a Miami Oriaté copied an entire Ifá book and replaced Orunmila's name with Changó throughout.

2. This song is asking Elegguá to ensure the bird will go to heaven for having given its life for the sacrifice. Those present pull on the skin

of their necks acknowledging that we all will die someday, just as surely as the bird is dying.

3. From the song for applying Epó (palm oil), "Palm oil soothes Ayalá, palm oil soothes." Ayalá is the oricha who constructs our orí, which in turn rules our destiny.

4. In his book *Religious Encounter and the Making of the Yoruba*, J.D.Y. Peel provides an outstanding account of how Christian missionaries, particularly those connected to the Anglican Church Missionary Society, created a Yoruba identity as well as the first Yoruba dictionaries in an attempt to standardize the language. As an interesting side note, this standardized Yoruba was constructed using Egba dialect with Oyó grammar. This is reminiscent of the mixing of languages that occurred at about the same time in Cuba.

5. While in Yorubaland there are some exceptions to this rule regarding reading only twelve odduns, the vast majority adhered to this practice which is the tradition in Cuba as well. An excellent description of a priest of Obatalá who read all sixteen signs and the verses he used can be found in William Bascom's book *Sixteen Cowries*. The book is also interesting in that it clearly depicts how only the one oricha speaks in the classical diloggún system and few references to any other orichas are to be found.

6. David Brown writes in his book *Santería Enthroned* that this washing and feeding amounted to a re-initiation of Adechina, but this is an error. Re-initiations are not performed in Lucumí Ifá and never were, with the possible exception of the Villalonga line, which was hermetically sealed off from the other branches of Ifá until well into the twentieth century. If a person could be re-initiated that easily, we would have people being re-initiated simply because they don't like the oddun they came with, or because they came osogbo or for any reason at all. Secondly, to be initiated in Lucumí Ifá, Odun/Olófin has to be present in the room, and Odun/Olófin hadn't been brought to Cuba yet. Finally, in Yorubaland, babalawos wash and feed their Ifás every year for the annual Ifá Festival as well as for other major ceremonies.

There is an account by elder babalawo Hermes Valera Ramirez (Otura Sa) in Heriberto Feraudy Espino's book *Macua* describing these events as an ebbó, which would be more accurate. This serves as an example of how ethnologists can come to erroneous, although usually well-meaning, conclusions and illustrates why their books need to be read with care rather than blindly accepted at face value.

That said, a few years back I did hear rumors of a case where a person was supposedly re-initiated because the new initiate had come with his godfather's sign Baba Eyiogbe. The godfather was terrified by this turn of events as the oddun speaks of betrayal on a massive scale on the part of the godchild (something which the godfather was said to have done to his own godfather), so the babalawos re-consecrated the new initiate's ekin nuts, and the divination was performed anew where the sign Ogunda Meyi appeared. If this even occurred, the person is and will always be a child of Baba Eyiogbe and nothing can change that. The oddun that appeared the second time, Ogunda Meyi (an oddun of harsh justice), was most likely Ifá's sentence on the godfather and the babalawos present for having committed such a travesty, either through lack of knowledge, fear, or greed.

7. An excellent description of the origin of Efunché's kariocha ceremony, including the war with opposing santera Obatero caused by the innovation can be found in *La División de la Habana* by Miguel W. Ramos.

8. Accounts of babalawos performing tasks such as shaving the head of the new initiate, which would later become the exclusive responsibility of the obá oriaté, the master of ceremonies for oricha initiations can be found in David Brown's *Santería Enthroned* and Lydia Cabrera's *Koeko Iyawó*.

9. Ño is an honorific title denoting great respect, and was almost exclusively used for those priests who came over from Africa.

Chapter Five: Lucumí

1. When a person is mounted or possessed by an oricha, they are not conscious of anything the oricha has said or done, and must be told later what occurred in their absence.

2. A well researched account of this war can be found in Miguel Ramos's paper *La División de la Habana*.

3. The famous ethnographer Fernando Ortiz lists Aña Bí as being a babalawo, although he is not remembered as such by the babalawo or drumming communities. Ortiz does not mention the fact that Atanda was a babalawo, so there is a chance he confused the two drumming priests.

4. Israel Molinaire, City of Matanzas historian, informed Miguel Ramos of an inspector's report that Adechina had been seen playing the batá drums in his cabildo on December 3, 1873. Personal communication between Israel Molinaire and Miguel Ramos reported in Ramos's paper *La División de la Habana*.

5. In his book *Santería Enthroned: Art, Ritual and Innovation in an Afro-Cuban Religion*, David Brown references letters written by Miguel Gomez claiming babalawos, including Tata Gaitán and Guillermo Castro went to drink water at the fount of Ortiz's library. It is interesting to note that Brown himself buys into this myth of a Yoruba purity, and therefore validity when he writes that Gaitán 'completed' his knowledge through the information he found in Ortiz's library (Brown, 2003).

6. William Bascom conducted extensive field studies in Yorubaland in 1937–38, 1950–51, 1960, and 1965 in the cities of Ifé, Meko, Oyó, Ilesa, Ilaro, Ilara, Abeokuta, Ibadan, Iseyin, Oke-Iho, Irawo, Ogbomoso, Osogbo, Sagamu, Ijebú Ode, Ondo, and a half dozen towns in Ekiti. Bascom became initiated into the Ifá and Ogboni cults as well. He and his wife-to-be Berta Montero also spent an entire year in Cuba and made several return visits during the ensuing years. Bascom was so meticulous that it took him thirty-one years to write *Ifá Divination: Communication Between Gods and Men in West Africa*, and twenty-nine

years to complete *Sixteen Cowries: Yoruba Divination from Africa to the New World.*

7. In *Obí Agbón: Lukumí Divination with Coconut,* which I believe to be the most accurate study on Obí divination, Ramos describes being present at a meeting with Abimbola in Puerto Rico, where Abimbola stated that he had been sent by the Ooni of Ilé Ifé specifically to recuperate some of what had been lost in Africa, and to promote greater understanding between African and New World practitioners as a religious institution, a culture, and as a people. Ramos claims Eddie Faiña (Yomí Yomí), Julio Ruíz (Ilarí), Roberto Boluffer (Ogundá Lení), and santera author Marta Morena Vega were also present, among others.

8. In fact, the religion is listed as one of the eight world religions along with Buddhism, Hinduism, Taoism, Confucianism, Judaism, Islam, and Christianity by Stephen Prothero in his book *God Is Not One.*

9. An account of how Olófin was brought to the US and the subsequent initiations can be found in David Brown's *Santería Enthroned.*

10. Fortunately, we have the book *Manual de Orihate* written by Nicolas Angarica, one of the handful of oriatés directly trained by the first professional oriaté Obadimeyi. This book authoritatively shows us that iworos, including the oriatés, who are the acknowledged experts in diloggún divination, held to these traditional limits as late as 1955. Angarica confirms these limits of the diloggún and past the twelfth letra all you have is the number of shells that have landed mouth up. Metanla meaning thirteen, merinla meaning fourteen, marunla meaning fifteen, and merindilogún meaning sixteen (Angarica, 1955). This is confirmed by Lydia Cabrera's informants from the 1940s and 1950s recorded in her classic *El Monte* as well as her other books (Cabrera, 1957). Because the diloggún is designed as a mouthpiece for the orichas and not Ifá it is extremely rare for these signs to appear in the first two throws, with odds lower than one in one thousand, and many iworos go through their entire lives without ever seeing these letras appear in consultation.

11. Again, we have Angarica's authoritative book showing that the Afro-Cuban tradition regarding reading the diloggún were actually interpreted as late as 1955, where the double signs were not read in the same form as Ifá. Instead, each sign of the double throw of the cowrie shells were interpreted. For example, if the sign Ogundá appeared followed by Odí, the iworo would give the advice from Ogundá followed by the advice associated with Odí.

12. For a detailed account sprinkled throughout with such experiences by a well-known oricha priest and drummer who came over in the Mariel Boatlift, see *Drumming for the Gods: The Life and Times of Felipe García Villamil, Santero, Palero, and Abakuá* by Maria Teresa Velez.

13. Informants for Lydia Cabrera mention babalawos having performed the tasks now conducted by the oriatés in the past as well as in Africa, which she mentions in her work *Koeko Iyawó*.

14. In his book *Santería Enthroned* David Brown cites the case of Jose Miguel Gomez Barbera, whose own 1929 initiation in Ocha was directed by babalawos who conducted the main ceremonies such as the shaving and ritual painting; even the itá was performed using the Table of Ifá instead of with the shells. It also appears some of the most important santeras of the time were present, such as Latuán and Tiburcia Sotolongo. Brown encountered this information in a letter Gomez had written to Radamés Corona on October 21, 1989. The fact remains though, that the oriaté became the universally accepted master of ceremonies of the initiation ceremonies by the end of the 1930s, most likely due to agreements with the prevailing babalawos of the time, such as Tata Gaitán.

Chapter Six: Orichas and Powers

1. This profound conversation between Bernardo Rojas and his son was told to David Brown by the elder babalawo Hermes Valera Ramírez in 1993.

2. Palo Monte is often mistakenly depicted as black magic and sorcery. Also referred to as La Regla Kongo, it is the religion hailing from the

Bantu or Congo areas of Africa. The fact that there is little imposed morality has led some to the confused conclusion that it is black magic. In fact, most practitioners, known as paleros, work for the good of their godchildren and clients. The palero works heavily with the Dead, who like the living, can be good, evil, or everything in between. Also, the nganga and the religion in general rely heavily on the palero's personal ethics.

3. Though the title Olófin does not seem to be commonly used any longer in Yorubaland, its existence is confirmed by E. Bolaji Idowu in his landmark book *Olodumare: God in Yoruba Belief* where he depicts Olófin as another name for Olodumare (Bolaji, 1995).

Chapter Seven: Initiations

1. This means, "The elder is making blindness pass away, the elder is making loss pass away."

2. According to some of Lydia Cabrera's informants, the elekes were traditionally only given when an oricha was calling for a person to be initiated as their priest or priestess and the person could not afford it. The initiates were then given their necklaces to appease the oricha until the person could acquire the means to become initiated. This is where the term medio asiento, or half-seated (initiated), came into use.

3. Warriors given by santeros are similar to warriors given by babalawos, though there are a couple of differences. One, the Elegguá they give doesn't come with a name or path until the person is fully initiated as a santera/o, if that is their path in the religion. The other difference is that only the babalawos can give Osun, which is an Ifá staff. There is more information regarding the differences between the Echu given by the babalawo and the Elegguá given by the oloricha in chapter six.

4. At the time of this agreement, the babalawo's tasks began with the consultation and ebbó de entrada, where Ifá would give his advice to the initiate-to-be. The iyefá from the divination would then be added in the secret mixture called the machuquillo to lend Orunmila's aché

to the ceremony. During one initiation as a santero my padrino, the famous oriaté Guillermo Diago (Obá Bí-ibaé), informed me that traditionally the babalawo would also use the ecuele to find out which otanes (stones) were acceptable to the orichas. The next day the babalawo would perform a short cleansing and blessing of the plants that were to be used to make the omiero in the ceremony, which is called making Osain. Later, the babalawo would add Ifá's blessing to the omiero itself. During the kariocha proper, the only official role the babalawo had was to present the razor to the initiate's head and then hand the razor to the oriaté to perform the head shaving. This act itself seems very much like a re-enactment of how the babalawos turned over a number of responsibilities to the oriatés. Finally, in the oddun Irete Untedí, Ifá warns that olorichas and babalawos need to unite or everybody will lose. This is a warning I take very seriously as it is my oddun from when I received Olokun.

Chapter Nine: Odduns

1. Traditionally, the manner in which the diloggún is read is in the form of combining the advice of the two letras that make up their combination odduns. In other words, if the combination Ogundá Oché is thrown, the oloricha will give advice from Ogundá followed by advice from Oché, but during the 1970s, as santeros began to get their hands on Ifá books we began seeing the diloggún being read like Ifá. This is far from traditional, and olorichas who do this are forced to omit a number of patakís that reveal embarrassing contradictions in their practices. These olorichas attempt to rationalize these contradictions by claiming the troublesome histories are not traditional, while all the while the very fact they are attempting to interpret the shells as Ifá is anything but traditional in the first place.

Chapter Eleven: Women and Feminine Power in Ifá

1. This is the traditional salute to an Ifá priest, "Sacrifice offered, sacrifice accepted, sacrifice is blessed." Often the rank of the priest is included as part of the salute. For example, "Oluwo iború, Oluwo iboya, Oluwo

ibocheché," or, "Oyugbona iború, Oyugbona iboya, Oyugbona ibocheché."

2. Just as in the case of the babalawo, the oddun from the Abo faca or kofá ceremony is considered to have been an interim oddun until the person passes through their second initiation, with the new oddun superceding the earlier one.

3. Accounts of these santeras and their babalawo husbands can be found in Miguel Ramos's *La Division de La Habana* and in David Brown's *Santeria Enthroned*.

4. In Africa, each oricha have their own enclosed grove or forest where secret ceremonies such as initiations occur. In Cuba these have been replaced with sealed rooms for practical reasons. Odun's vast importance is seen in the fact that the name of the initiation shrine for Ifá is Igbo Odun (elided together as Igbodun) instead of Igbo Orunmila or Igbo Ifá.

5. Although the Yoruba religious capital of Ilé Ifé, the current Araba (highest-ranking babalawo) and the Awishé (Official Spokesperson and Inspector General) Wande Abimbola now support the idea of initiating female Ifá priests, it appears that this may not have always been the case. Accounts by Ikulomi Djisovi Eason, scholar and priest of Hevioso associated with Oyotunji African Village in South Carolina point to a recent change in the attitudes of the Ifá hierarchy in Ilé Ifé. In the book, *Orisa Devotion as World Religion,* Dr. Eason recounts how in 1992 the King of Oyotunji Adefunmi, under pressure from women at Oyotunji to allow them to be initiated as Ifá priests, was forced to go to Benin to initiate them because Ilé Ifé still didn't permit it at that time.

Chapter Twelve: Tata Gaitán

1. Though we often refer to different lineages as ramas, practically speaking, Cuban Ifá consists of only one rama with different lines interlocking and collaborating. It is very common for babalawos to have padrinos from different lineages.

2. Although Oluguere and Ño Cardenas were born in Africa they were both initiated to Ifá in Cuba by Adechina, and were therefore brothers in Ifá. The fact that Oluguere and Ño Cardenas were African born has led some to assume they had been initiated as babalawos before coming to Cuba, but this is not the case. Thus, the Tata Gaitán rama of Ifá is actually itself a branch of the Adechina rama.

Epilogue: One Babalawo's Story

1. Although our lineage is named after Tata Gaitán, our roots go back to Adechina, who was Tata Gaitán's grandfather and oyugbona in Ifá.

2. My Ifá lineage starts with Adechina, who brought Ifá to Cuba from Africa. Adechina (Obara Meyi) initiated Oluguery (Oyekun Meyi) to Ifá. Oluguery initiated Tata Gaitán (Ogundá Fún) with Adechina serving as the oyugbona. Tata Gaitán made Ifá to Alfredo Rivero (Otrupon Bekonwá), who initiated Octavio Ayala (Oché Fún), who made Ifá to Lazaro Sanchez (Irete Untelú), who made Ifá to Erminio Ogbe Funfunlo de Santa Cruz del Norte. He initiated Domingo Sanchez (Ogbe Che), who initiated my Padrino Pete Rivera (Odí Ogundá), who then initiated me.

3. The elekes (collars in Spanish and necklaces in English) are usually the first initiation received from an oloricha. This puts the initiate under the protection and care of the oloricha's orichas and makes them a member of their ilé or oricha house. Only olorichas should give the elekes.

Glossary

Aberinkulá: Unconsecrated. Most often used to refer to unconsecrated drums.

Abo faca, Awo faca: Preliminary male initiation into the Ifá sect, giving them one hand of Ifá. Also known as *Mano de Orula,* or Hand of Orula.

Achá: Cigar.

Aché, Ashé: Power, energy. The living power that permeates everything in the universe.

Áché O: Translated to "may it be so" or "may it come to pass." Said at the end of requests to an oricha or eggun.

Achedá: Originally Orula's first disciple. Also title for the highest-ranking priest in Cuba. Tata Gaitán is the only person who was ever installed as Achedá in Cuba.

Acho: Cloth.

Ada: Machete.

Adié: Hen.

Adimú: An offering to an oricha, often foods, drinks, or a favorite dish cooked especially for them.

Adimú Oricha: Oricha that is received without having to be initiated as a priestess or priest. Can also be received after initiation.

Agogó: Type of bell used in religious music or when talking to certain orichas such as Obatalá and Oduduwa.

Ahijada, ahijado: Godchild. A person who has received one or more initiations from a particular priest.

Aikú, Arikú: Health, literally means lack of death.

Aiyé: The world or this earth.

Akukó: Rooster.

Alagua lagua: Highly respected and acknowledged elder. Sometimes spelled agua lagua, lagualagua, alagua lagua, or agbalagba.

Aleyo: A person who has not been initiated as an oricha or Ifá priest. Meaning stranger, it refers to those who are a stranger to the igbodún or initiation room. Those who have not been through the initiation process.

Añá: Oricha of the drums. Drums that have been consecrated.

Anagó: The Lucumí language.

Apere: The container Orula's ekin nuts are housed. Considered to be female and a type of womb enclosing Ifá.

Apetebí: Female initiates in Ifá. Caretaker of Orunmila.

Apetebí Ayafá: Apetebí who has gone through a deeper initiation receiving sixteen ekin nuts and is considered the wife of Ifá.

Araba: Ceiba or silk cotton tree (*Ceiba pentandra*). Considered the most powerful and venerated of all trees. In some cities in Africa, such as Ilé Ifé, Araba is the title of the highest ranking babalawo in that Yoruba nation.

Arun, Ano: Sickness. One of the possible osogbos (negative manifestations) of an oddun that can come up during and osode or Ifá consultation.

Ataná: Candle.

Atefá: Term used for the initiation of a person as a babalawo. Sometimes used to describe divining using the Table of Ifá, though simply tefá is more common.

Awó: Secret. Proper name of any person who has been initiated as an Ifá priest.

Ayalá: The oricha who constructs the orí (head). Has control over the quality of each head, and is important that he be propitiated.

Baba Eyiobge: An Ifá oddun. It is the most senior of all odduns, hence the honorific term Baba or father in the name. It is considered the father of all the odduns.

Babalawo: Father of the Secrets. Most commonly used term for a priest initiated into the mysteries of Ifá and properly trained. In the strictest definitions it applies only to a person who has initiated someone into the mysteries of Ifá.

Batá: Lucumí sacred drums consisting of three hourglass-shaped drums named the Iyá, the okónkolo, and the itótele. Batá drumming is very complex. The drums talk to the orichas with each of the deities having several of their own rhythms. The drums also talk with each other through calls where they communicate upcoming changes in the rhythm. These drums are consecrated to the oricha of drumming Añá and drummers are sworn to the drums as well.

Cabildo: Organized in the form of the Spanish cofradías under the patronage of the church. The cabildos de nación were mutual aid organizations for the various African ethnicities. In the early days much of their work was centered around such activities as buying their brethren out of slavery. Later the cabildos became a means to preserve, organize, and practice the Afro-Cuban religions such as Santería, Palo, and Abakuá in secret.

Calabash, Calabaza: A large, gourd-like shell often cut in half. Traditionally used to contain orichas or powers. The universe is often pictures as an immense calabash.

Carga: Literally meaning load. A group of special ingredients used by babalawos to fill, empower, and give birth to certain orichas and powers such as Echu, Olokun, and Oduduwa.

Ceiba: Araba in Lucumí. Silk cotton tree (*Ceiba pentandra*). Considered most powerful and venerated of all trees. See Araba.

Changó: The oricha of thunder, fire, dance, and drums.

Cuanaldo: A ceremony performed on babalawos some time after their initiation as an Ifá priest. Confers upon the babalawo the right to initiate others into Ifá and the ability to sacrifice four-legged animals.

Cuje: Spanish term for a thin stick, used in the iyoye ceremony to strike the neophyte babalawo.

Diloggún: Divination method used by iworos. The diloggún uses sixteen consecrated cowry shells. The name comes from the Yoruba word Merindilogun meaning sixteen. Of the sixteen letras or signs, only twelve can be read. If one of the other four signs appears, it means the oricha is ordering the iworo to send the person to a babalawo, as the situation requires the client to be seen with Ifá.

Derecho: Ritual payment for work done by a santera, santero, or babalawo.

Dundún: Black.

Ebbó: An offering or sacrifice used to propitiate an eggún or oricha. Usually to cleanse, protect, or ensure good fortune to a person. There are many types of ebbós ranging from a candle or fruits to the sacrifice of an animal. Some ebbós can be complex undertakings.

Ebbó Katero: An extremely powerful ebbó performed using the Table of Ifá.

Echu: The oricha who owns all roads and doors in life, and is Orula's most trusted assistant.

Ecuele: Divining chain used by a babalawo during a divination session to access prayers, chants, and rituals. It is comprised of eight discs connected to each other by a chain, and is considered the servant, or messenger, of Ifá.

Edduara: Thunder stone. This is as teardrop shaped stone that is said to be embedded in the ground wherever lightning strikes. Lightning is said to be caused by Changó throwing them to earth, often as a punishment. In Yorubaland, priests of Changó are called whenever lightning kills someone so they can remove the edduara and cleanse the body.

Efún: A kind of white chalk used in ceremonies and in offerings, and often called by its Spanish name cascarilla. In Cuba and the United States it is often made from eggshells.

Eggun: The dead. It is often used more specifically to mean the dead within one's own family in blood and/or religion.

Eiyelé: Pigeon.

Ekin, equin, ikin, ekines: The nut of the Opé Ifá or Oil Palm of Ifá (*Elaesis guineensis idolatica*) used in the worship of Orula and to perform deep Ifá divination.

Eledá: Creator. Is associated with our deepest consciousness. See orí.

Elegán: An initiation performed in some parts of Yorubaland on men without Odun being present. These people are not recognized as babalawos by Lucumí babalawos, and traditionally are only allowed to divine for themselves and their immediate family. They are also not allowed to initiate anyone into the religion.

Eleke, ileke: Bead necklace (collar in Spanish). Also an initiation performed by iworos and not babalawos. The initiation and neck-laces put the person under the care and protection of the iworo's orichas. The iworo then becomes the godparent of the elekes' initiate, and they are formally a member of the iworo's ilé.

Elerí Ikúin: Witness to Destiny in Creation. Title of Orula who is the only oricha allowed to witness the creation of the universe. Also refers to Orula's role as the only oricha allowed to witness the choosing of a person's destiny before coming to this world.

Elese: Meaning at the feet of. Usually referred to when asking from whom an iré or osogbos comes from.

Epó: Palm oil.

Ese Ifá: Parables in the form of verses or poems. A mnemonic device allowing the student to learn quicker and easier.

Ewo: Prohibitions forbidding a person to eat certain foods, to wear certain types of clothes, or other provisions for the well-being of that person.

Eyo Ifá: The ese Ifá in narrative form. The African equivalent of the itán or patakí in Cuba.

Fundamentos: Foundational objects pertaining to the religion, such as the stones or ekines in which the orichas or Orula lives.

Funfún: White.

Guerreros: The Warriors often used for protection. They include Echu, Oggún, Ochossi, and Osun if received from a babalawo, and Elegguá, Oggún, and Ochossi if received from an iworo. This is because only babalawos can give Echu or the Ifá staff known as Osun (Ayagún in Lucumí).

Ibae: A salutation for someone who has passed away.

Iború, Iboya, Ibocheché: Ifá salute meaning "sacrifice offered, sacrifice received, sacrifice is effective." Also the name of three women who saved Orula from a pit in the ground where he had been trapped for days.

Iche: Works done to help a person with a particular situation.

Iddé: Bracelet usually pertaining to one of the orichas.

Idefá: Bracelet made of green and yellow beads received during the kofá or Abo faca initiation. Identifies the person as child of Orula protecting them from Death, due to the pact between Orula and Death.

Ifá: Highest form of divination in the religion. Another name for Orula/Orunmila, the oricha of wisdom, knowledge, and divination.

Igba: Container.

Igbabo: Believers. A derisive term used by oricha worshippers in Yorubaland to poke fun at Christians for having a god who needs to be believed in.

Igba Odun: Calabash of Odun (the Supreme Being). Sometimes referred to as Igba Iwa (Calabash of All Existence). Indispensable for initiating a new babalawo. Also known as Olófin.

Igbo: Sacred grove belonging to an oricha where secret ceremonies such as initiations take place. In Yorubaland, each oricha has its own where priests of other orichas are not welcome. The only exception is for obás, babalawos, and apetebís, who are free to enter any sacred grove.

Igbodún: Originally, Odun's sacred grove where Ifá initiations were carried out. Became the name for the room where oricha priests are initiated in Cuba.

Ikú: Death. One of the principle osogbos (negative) of an oddun. Also the deity of death.

Ilé: House. Used to denote an oricha house where an iworo or babalawo live and work as well as the religious family itself.

Ilé Ifé: City-State in Yorubaland considered to be the ancestral homeland of all the Yoruba as well as the spiritual capital. Also called simply Ifé.

Iré: Blessing, benefit, or good fortune. Most often used in connection with divination.

Irofá: Tapper of Ifá. Tapped on the edge of the Table of Ifá during prayers whenever working with it.

Iruke: A beaded horsetail switch that is the emblem of a babalawo. Also used to cleanse people of negativity and cover the ekines when outside Orula's receptacle and not being used.

Itá: A ceremonial deep divination performed during a major initiation.

Italero: A person who is expert in the use of the diloggún, in particular the obá oriaté.

Itán: The mythic parables of Ifá. Also known as patakí.

Iwá: Character, existence. Sometimes used for destiny.

Iwá Pele, Iwá Cuele: Character brought into balance through the careful and thoughtful application of a thorough knowledge of our destiny.

Iworo: An oricha priest. Also referred to as an oloricha or santera/o.

Iyanifá: Female Ifá priest. Not recognized by Afro-Cuban babalawos or in a number of regions of Yorubaland because an initiation without Odin or Olófin present is not considered valid. They appear to be a recent innovation as the earliest reference to them in Yorubaland appear to date from the 1970s. It is interesting to note that there are far more American Iyanifás than there are in Africa.

Iyawó: A recently initiated oricha priest, meaning bride of the oricha. The initiate remains at this position for a year and a week after the initiation and must follow many prohibitions. These restrictions are intended to keep them in a state of purity for the first year.

Iyefá: Ifá powder used on the Table of Ifá to divine with or make ebbós with. Can also be marked with odduns on the Table of Ifá, and when accompanied by the proper incantations can be used for a wide variety of purposes.

Iyoreosún: Powder used on the Table of Ifá to mark odduns during divination. The powder is also used during the ebbó katero to cleanse and strengthen a person. At times a babalawo will mark odduns in the powder to cause the effects of tat oddun to come to pass.

Iyoyé: The closing ceremonies during the initiation of a new babalawo. Best known for the re-enactment of events in the life of the ancient initiate Akala, where the new initiate is struck repeatedly with cujes by other babalawos.

Jicara: Pronounced HEE-cah-rah. A gourd-like shell used in the New World that is usually cut in half with the halves used as containers to hold water, ekines, or other small objects.

Kariocha: The initiation ceremony of an oricha priest (santero). Often referred to as "making ocha."

Kebori Eledá: Translates to "to put ebbó to Orí Eledá." Also referred to by its Spanish name rogación de la cabeza. A ceremony that cleanses, strengthens, and propitiates a person's orí.

Kuanado, Cuanaldo: Ceremony granting the initiate the ability to use a knife for sacrifices and allows them to initiate other babalawos. Usually the first initiation received after making Ifá, or being initiated as a babalawo.

Kofá: A woman's initiation into Ifá, giving her the rank of Apetebí Ifá, or caretaker of Ifá.

Lalafia: General well-being. An iré or positive aspect of an oddun.

Limpieza: Spanish word for a cleansing.

Letra: Spanish slang term for oddun. Literally means letter, as in a letter from the alphabet.

Lucumí: Name used in Cuba to identify people who hailed from various nations to later become known as the Yoruba, as well as some of the surrounding peoples. Also refers to the religion, culture, and language in general.

Madrina: Godmother. Person who initiates godchildren into her ilé.

Maferefún: Praise be to. Usually said to orichas.

Meyi, Olodu: An oddun where the right and left sides are identical. Considered to be senior to the rest of the odduns.

Mo iwá fun oniwá: Respect the character a person is born with.

Moducué: I thank you.

Moyuba: I salute you. A prayer saluting Olófin, our familial and spiritual ancestors, the orichas, and is used at the beginning of every ritual.

Nganga: A container, often a cauldron,containing special plants, animals, dirt, bones, and the spirit of a deceased person used in rituals and ceremonies. Also referred to as a prenda, Spanish for jewel.

Obá: King.

Obátalá: Father of the orichas and representative of Olófin on earth. Rules over the mind, judgement, and peace. In Ayáguna path he is a warrior who ferments revolution.

Obe: Knife.

Obí: Divination using four pieces of coconut. Used to elicit yes or no answers from the egguns and orichas.

Obí agbon: Coconut. In Africa they used kola nuts to elicit a yes or no answer in divination, but because they were difficult to get in Cuba they began using coconut as a substitute.

Ocha: Name for the Lucumí religion, shortened from *La Regla Ocha* or Rule of the Orichas. Also initiation of an oricha priest, short for making Ocha, and for any of the orichas one can be initiated to as a priest. Also called Kariocha or Yoko Ocha.

Oché: The name of an oddun in Ifá and diloggún.

Ochossi: Oricha of the Hunt and Justice. Received as part of the initiation known as the Guerreros.

Ochún: The oricha who rules over the fresh waters, sensuality, and matters of the heart. Also considered Queen of the Witches.

Oddun: One of the 256 signs in Ifá. Everything in the universe was born in one of the odduns and includes the totality of human experience. Each oddun has plants, stories, proverbs, advice, offerings, and its own paths of Echu.

Oddun Toyale: During an osode or Ifá consultation, this is the first and main oddun or Ifá sign. It contains the bulk of the advice Ifá has for the person.

Odun: One of the manifestations of the Supreme Being. Considered to be the most accessible of these manifestations, Odun is also known as Olófin. She is received by the most elder of the babalawos and is indispensable for initiation of Ifá priests.

Ofo: Loss. One of the principle osogbos (negative) aspects of an oddun.

Ofún: The name of an oddun in Ifá and diloggún.

Ogbogba: Balance, equilibrium.

Oggún: Oricha of War and the Blacksmith of the orichas. Received as part of the Guerrero initiation.

Ogundá: The name of an oddun in Ifá and diloggún.

Olodumare:: One of three manifestations of the Supreme Being.

Olófin: One of three manifestations of the Supreme Being.

Olofista: A babalawo who has received Olófin (Odun). The highest rank of babalawos. Also known as Omo Odun, Obá Kolaba, or Omo Kolaba Olófin.

Olokun: The immensely powerful oricha who rules over the depths of the seas.

Olori Oricha: Meaning the oricha that is owner of the head. The tutelary oricha.

Oloricha: One who has oricha. An oricha priest. Also known as an iworo or santera/o.

Olorun: The Supreme Being associated with the sun.

Olubo Borotiri Baba Ebbó: Father of all ebbó. This is a massive series of ebbó, or offerings, performed for the entire world by groups of babalawos just before the New Year as part of the Apertura del Ano, or Opening of the Year rituals. Offerings are made to the orichas, the rivers, the sea, the moon, the sun, the other world, the dawn, the cemetery, and so on, to ensure the well-being of everyone in the world.

Oluwo: A babalawo initiated as an oloricha or oricha priest before initiated as a babalawo.

Oluwo Siwayú: An initiatory father or Godfather in Ifá. Often shortened to oluwo.

Omi: Water.

Omi tutu: Cool water.

Omiero: Consecrated water made with a number of plants sacred to the orichas through a long intricate ceremony. The herbal concoction usually prepared during initiations.

Omo: Child.

Omolu: Short for Omo Oluwo or Children of the Lords. The term used to denote the combination of odduns where the right and left sides are not identical. Considered the children and assistants of the Meyis. See Meyis.

Omo Odun: A babalawo who has received Odun (Olófin).

Ona: Path or road, often used to describe the different paths a particular oddun can take.

Ooni: Ruler of the Yoruba city-state of Ifé. In theory, they rule over all Yoruba nations.

Opón: The Table of Ifá. A round tablet used for deep divination.

Ori, Erí: Head. Taken from Oyó dialect of the Yoruba language. Personal deity each of us has, as well as our innermost consciousness. Rules our destiny, personality, and talents. Extremely powerful and the orichas cannot act for or against us without the permission of our orí. Ori's power is alluded to in the title Orí Eledá (Eledá meaning Creator), which reveals Orí to be a creator in its own right. There is also an archetypal Orí, an immensely powerful deity ruling over the Orís of everything, including the orichas. This archetypal Orí is received only by elder babalawos who have already received Olófin.

Orí Acueré: The archetypal orí that rules over everything having an orí whether it is an oricha, a human being, or other being.

Orí Inú: Inner head. Formal name for the spiritual aspect of our orí.

Oriaté, Obá Oriaté: Master of Ceremonies for oricha initiations. Is extremely knowledgeable in all aspects of oricha worship and is second only to babalawos.

Oricha: Goddess or God. The deities and emissaries of Olófin (God) who rule over the forces of nature and human endeavors.

Oriki: Prayers of praise.

Oró iyinle: Deep words. Most often seen in prayers and songs.

Orula: The oricha of omniscience, wisdom, knowledge and divination. Also known as Orunmila and Ifá.

Orun: The Other World. Sometimes referred to as heaven, particularly when speaking to outsiders.

Orunmila: The oricha of omniscience, wisdom, knowledge, and divination. Also known as Orula and Ifá.

Osí adié: Young male chicken.

Osode: An Ifá consultation.

Osogbo: Misfortune. Most often used in connection with divination.

Osun: Ifá staff usually received when a person receives the Warriors from a babalawo. Messenger of Olófin, watches over the well-being of the initiate and will fall over to give warning of impending danger.

Otán: Consecrated stones to the orichas.

Owe: Proverb (refrán in Spanish).

Otí: Rum.

Oyale/Yale: When oddun comes with iré, or positivity, and with blessings. Yale means the blessings are firmly planted and strong.

Oyugbona: Assistant priest or second Madrina or padrino in a major initiation. Translates to "one who clears the road." Often performs as much or more of the training of initiate than main godparent.

Padrino: Godfather. Person who initiates godchildren into his ilé.

Paraldo: Ceremony performed by babalawos to separate an unwanted spirit from a person.

Pataki: A mythic history or parable associated with the odduns in Ifá.

Pinaldo: A ceremony that can be performed after a person has been initiated as an oricha priest. Oggún's diloggún are received and is considered a confirmation of their initiation. Some say the ceremony is derived from the re-initiations performed by Latuán, Efunche, and Obadimeyi. Others, pointing to the name and the claim the ceremony confirms the right to sacrifice four-legged animals, believe the ceremony is an attempt to copy the babalawo's Cuanaldo ceremony.

Popopún: A bed or bedding. Part of a song used when spreading feathers over the oricha after a sacrifice. "*Popopún mi, popopún mi iye* (my blanket, my blanket of feathers)."

Pukua: Red.

Rama: A branch or lineage of the religion.

Refrán: Proverb (*owe* in Lucumí).

Rogación de la cabeza: Prayer for the head. Spanish word for the *keborí eledá* ceremony used to cleanse, feed, and fortify the *orí*.

Santero: Oricha priest.

Sarayeye: A type of cleansing where plants, animals, or other items are passed over the body to pick up any negativity before being offered to an oricha.

Sopera: A soup tureen. Often used to house the orichas.

Tablero de Ifá/Table of Ifá: The opón or Ifá divination tray.

Tambor: Spanish for drum. Most commonly name used for a drumming ceremony.

Teja: Spanish for roof tile. Used to worship the eggun after passing through ceremonies and being marked with certain odduns.

Testigos: Spanish for witness. Used as a type of slang term for the two odduns that are obtained after the main oddun, which expands on the advice of the oddun toyale. These witnesses are used to ascertain whether a person has come in iré or osogbo.

Wemilere: Drumming ceremony for eggun or the orichas.

Yemayá: The oricha of the Seas. Name meaning "mother whose children are the fish." As the Mother of the World, Yemayá rules over maternity and is known for her nurturing nature although she can also be a fierce Warrior and witch.

Bibliography

Abimbola, Wande and Ivor Miller. *Ifá Will Mend Our Broken World: Thoughts on Yoruba Religion and Culture in Africa and the Diapora*. Roxbury, MA: Aim Books, 1997.

Abraham, Roy Clive. *Dictionary of Modern Yoruba*. London: University of London Press, 1958.

Angarica, Nicolas Valentin. *Manual De Orihate: Religion Lucumi*. Havana, Cuba, 1955.

Arango, Pedro, et. al. *Iwe ni Iyewó ni Ifá Orunmila*. Havana, 1940.

Ayorinde, Christine. "Santería in Cuba: Tradition and Transformation." In *The Yoruba Diaspora in the Atlantic World*, edited by Toyin Falola and Matt D. Childs. Bloomington: Indiana University Press, 2005.

Bascom, William. *Ifá divination: Communication between Gods and Men in West Africa*. Bloomington: Indiana University Press, 1969.

———. "La Religion Africaine au Nouveau Monde." In *Les religions africaines traditionnelles*. Paris: Éditions du Seuil, 1965, 119–127.

———. *Sixteen Cowries: Yoruba Divination from Africa to the New World*. Bloomington: Indiana University Press, 1980.

Beier, Ulli. *Return of the Gods: The Sacred Art of Susanne Wenger*. Cambridge: Cambridge University Press, 1975.

Bolívar Aróstegui, Natalia. *Los Orichas en Cuba.* Havana: Ediciones Unión, Unión de Escritores y Artistas de Cuba, 1990.

Brown, David. *Santeria Enthroned: Art, Ritual and Innovation in an Afro-Cuban Religion.* Chicago: University of Chicago Press, 2003.

Cabrera, Lydia. *Anagó: Vocabulario Lucumí. El Yoruba Que Se Habla en Cuba.* Miami: Cabrera y Rojas, [1954] 1970.

——. *El Monte: Igbo-Finda, Ewe Orisha-Vititi Nfinda, Notas Sobre las Religiones, la Magia, las Supersticiones y el Folklore de los Negros Criollos y del Pueblo de Cuba.* Miami: Ediciones Universal, [1957] 1975.

——. *Koeko Iyawó: aprende novicia: pequeño tratado de regla lucumí.* Miami: Ediciones Universal, 1980.

Concordia, Maria "Oggun Gbemi." *The Anagó Language of Cuba.* Raleigh: Lulu Press, 2012.

Demanget, Magali. "El Precio de La Tradición: En Torno a Los Intercambios Entre Riqueza Económica y Espiritual En La Comunidad Mazateca Huautla de Jiménez, Oaxaca." *Cuadernos de Trabajo, Instituto de Investigaciones Histórico-Sociales, Universidad Veracruzana* Vol 6 (2000).

Dice Ifá. Havana, 2007.

Dictionary of the Yoruba Language. Lagos: Church Missionary Society Bookshop, [1911] 1937.

Drewal, Margaret Thompson. *Yoruba Ritual: Performers, Play, Agency.* Bloomington. Indiana University Press, 1992.

Drewal, Margaret Thompson and Henry John Drewel. "An Ifa Diviner's Shrine in Ijebuland in *UCLA James S. Coleman African Studies Center,* 1983." *UCLA James S. Coleman African Studies Center* 16.2: 61–100.

Eason, Ikulomi Djisovi. "Historicizing Ifá Culture in Oyotunji African Village." In *Orisa Devotion as World Religion: The Globalization of Yoruba Religious Culture,* ed. Jacob Kehinde Olupona and Terry Rey, 278–85. Madison: University of Wisconsin Press, 2008.

Eltis, David. "The Diaspora of Yoruba Speakers, 1650–1865: Dimensions and Implications." In *The Yoruba Diaspora in the Atlantic World,* ed. Toyin Falola and Matt D. Childs, 29–31. Bloomington: University of Indian Press, 2004.

Feraudy Espino, Heriberto. *Macua*. Santo Domingo, República Domini-
cana: Editora Manatí, 2002.

Gonzales-Wippler, Migene. *Santería: The Religion: Faith, Rites, Magic*. St.
Paul, MN: Llewellyn Publications, 2002.

Idowu, E. Bolaji. *Olodumare: God in Yoruba Belief*. New York: Frederick
A. Praeger, 1963.

Johnson, James. *Yoruba Heathenism*. Exeter: J. Townsend Press, 1899.

Johnson, Samuel. *The History of the Yorubas*. Lima, OH: CSS, [1921]
1997.

Lovejoy, Henry B. *The Proyecto Orunmila Texts of Osha-Ifá in Regla, Cuba*.
Studies in the History of the African Diapora-Documents 3 (2002): 1–3.

Maupoil, Bernard. *La Géomancie à l'Ancienne Côte des Esclaves*. Paris:
Institut d'Enthnologie, [1943] 1988.

Moreno Vega, Marta. "The Dynamic Influence of Cubans, Puerto
Ricans, and African Americans in the Growth of Ocha in New York
City." In *Orisa Devotion as World Religion: The Globalization of Yoruba
Religious Culture*, ed. by Jacob Kehinde Olupona and Terry Rey, 330.
Madison: University of Wisconsin Press, 2008.

Murphy, Joseph M. *Santería: An African Religion in America*. Boston:
Beacon Press, 1989.

Obairawo, "Lukumí ifa book unveiled and authenticated," Diaspora
Orisha Network (blog), January 29, 2008. http://diasporaorishanet-
work.yuku.com/reply/2881/Lukum-ifa-book-unveiled-and-
authenticated#reply-2881.

Oyotunji African Village. www.oyotunji.org/historical-timeline.html.

Palmie, Stephan. *The Cooking of History: How Not to Study Afro-Cuban
Religion*. Chicago: University of Chicago Press, 2013.

Peel, J. D. Y. *Religious Encounter and the Making of the Yoruba*. Bloomington: Indiana University Press, 2003.

Perez-Puelles, Froilan. *Tratado de Oddun de Ifa: Su Oráculo Completo*.
Havana.

Prothero, Stephen R. *God Is Not One: The Eight Rival Religions That Run
the World*. New York: HarperOne, 2011.

Ramos, Miguel W. *"La Division de La Habana: Territorial Conflict and Cultural Hegemony in the Followers of Oyo Lukumi Religion, 1850s-1920s"* in *Cuban Studies 34* (2003): 38–70.

———. *Obí Agbón: Lukumí Divination with Coconut*. Miami: Eleda.org Publications, 2012, 432–441.

———. *Orí Eledá Mí ó... Si Mi Cabeza No Me Vende*. Miami: Eleda.org Publications, 2011.

———. *The Empire Beats On: Oyó, Batá Drums and Hegemony in Nineteenth Century Cuba*. Masters Thesis, 2000.

Reid, Michele. "The Yoruba in Cuba." In *The Yoruba Diaspora in the Atlantic World*, ed. Toyin Falola and Matt D. Childs. Bloomington: Indiana University Press, 2004.

Sosa, Juan. "La Santería: An Integrating Mythological Worldview in a Disintegrating Society." In *Orisa Devotion as World Religion: The Globalization of Yoruba Religious Culture*, ed. Jacob Kehinde Olupona and Terry Rey, 378. Madison: University of Wisconsin Press, 2008.

Tratado Enciclopedico de Ifa. Havana.

Velez, Maria Teresa. *Drumming for the Gods: The Life and Times of Felipe García Villamil, Santero, Palero, and Abakuá*. Philadelphia: Temple University Press, 2000.

Verger, Pierre. "Grandeur et Décadence du Culte de Ìyámi Òsòròngà (Ma Mère la Sorcière) Chez les Yoruba." *Journal de la Société des Africanistes*. 35.1 (1965): 141–243.

———. *Notes sur le culte des Orisha et Vodoun, à Bahia, la Baie de tous les Saints au Brésil, et à l'ancienne côte des Esclaves*. Dakar: IFAN, 1957.

Wheeler, John. "Information, Physics, Quantum: The Search for Links." In *Complexity, Entropy, and the Physics of Information: The Proceedings of the 1988 Workshop on Complexity, Entropy, and the Physics of Information Held May-June, 1989, in Santa Fe, New Mexico*, ed. Wojciech Hubert Zurek. Boulder: Westview Press and the Perseus Books Group. 1990.

Zizzi, P. A. "Emergent consciousness: from the early universe to our mind." In *NeuroQuantology*. 3 (2003): 295-311. http://arxiv.org/abs/gr-qc/0007006.

Index

To Write to the Author

If you wish to contact the author or would like more information about this book, please write to the author in care of Llewellyn Worldwide Ltd. and we will forward your request. Both the author and publisher appreciate hearing from you and learning of your enjoyment of this book and how it has helped you. Llewellyn Worldwide Ltd. cannot guarantee that every letter written to the author can be answered, but all will be forwarded. Please write to:

Frank Baba Eyiogbe
℅ Llewellyn Worldwide
2143 Wooddale Drive
Woodbury, MN 55125-2989

Please enclose a self-addressed stamped envelope for reply,
or $1.00 to cover costs. If outside the U.S.A., enclose
an international postal reply coupon.

Many of Llewellyn's authors have websites with additional information and resources. For more information, please visit our website at http://www.llewellyn.com